RISING
WITH
JESUS

DONALD W. PATTERSON

RISING WITH JESUS

*God Pleasing Prayers
to Start Your Day*

XULON PRESS

Xulon Press
2301 Lucien Way #415
Maitland, FL 32751
407.339.4217
www.xulonpress.com

© 2020 by Donald W. Patterson

All rights reserved solely by the author. The author guarantees all contents are original and do not infringe upon the legal rights of any other person or work. No part of this book may be reproduced in any form without the permission of the author. The views expressed in this book are not necessarily those of the publisher.

Unless otherwise indicated, Scripture quotations taken from the Holy Bible, New International Version (NIV). Copyright © 1973, 1978, 1984, 2011 by Biblica, Inc.™. Used by permission. All rights reserved.

Printed in the United States of America.

ISBN-13: 978-1-6305-0720-6

DEDICATION

I dedicate this book to:

God who speaks to us through his word every day and loves it when we speak back to him, to my wife, Mary, who prays often to God in the secret place and encourages many through texted prayers when they go through hard times, to Amory Stephenson, who worked tirelessly to make this book a reality, and to all my Christian friends who have learned to pray God's thoughts back to him by walking with me in Daily Prayer.

JANUARY 1

Therefore, remember that formerly you ... were separate from Christ, excluded from citizenship in Israel and foreigners to the covenants of the promise, without hope and without God in the world. But now in Christ Jesus you who once were far away have been brought near by the blood of Christ. —Ephesians 2:1-13

Dear Jesus,
I sometimes forget that there was a time that I was lost without you in the world. In those times my contentment lags and I get disappointed with life because I live by my expectations of what I can get from this temporal world. But then you give me words like these in Ephesians 2 that remind me that I once was lost, without hope and without you in the world. Now, I remember that I have so much right now to be thankful for as a child of God with hope and peace. And to think that it took your death to give me this–ties me forever to you in loyalty. There is no other god that boasts of dying so that his subjects might truly live. In the new year I live in hope and peace. That gives me a lot to look forward to. AMEN

To be without God is to be lost in the jungle where every being you encounter wants to eat you and all you have for help is your own panicked mind.

Additional Readings: Exodus 3,4, Joshua 1, Matthew 28:20, Romans 8:18-39

JANUARY 2

Do not take revenge, my dear friends, but leave room for God's wrath, for it is written: "It is mine to avenge; I will repay," says the Lord. On the contrary: "If your enemy is hungry, feed him; if he is thirsty, give him something to drink. —Romans 12:19

Dear Jesus,
You modeled this word from the Holy Spirit perfectly. In grace you kept going back to get your wayward disciples without rejecting them. From the cross you forgave those murdering you. But me? I stumble and struggle. A big part of me wants to see all bullies fall into grave trouble. The pain they cause magnifies my sense of justice. I naturally want them to pay for their wrongs. But your love and redemption is sublimely more powerful, putting justice back in its cage. Fill me with your supernatural love so completely that I forgive those who have hurt or ignored me. Make me not wish any negative experience on them. But instead, help me seek to bless their lives in creative ways. I am yours. Change me into the peaceful, redemptive person that you are.
AMEN

Christ forgave everyone living with him when he walked the earth. Now, through us, he wants to forgive everyone living today.

Additional Readings: Lev 19:18, Proverbs 20:22, Proverbs 24:29, Deut. 32:35, Genesis 50:15-21, 1 Samuel 26:5-11

JANUARY 3

I pray that you, being rooted and established in love, may have power, together with all the Lord's holy people, to grasp how wide and long and high and deep is the love of Christ. —Ephesians 3:17-18

Dear Jesus,
Today, I willingly lay aside all my requests that you fix this or that in my life or in the lives of those I love. Instead, according to your word above, I ask with Paul, one thing: enlarge your love and power in my heart, so that I grasp more than ever before, how real and powerful that love is to make me secure, to give me peace and hope, to enable me to want to be there for other people, even those who irritate me, and to fill me to overflowing with love for everyone.
AMEN

You don't have what it takes to know the depth and breadth of God's love. This you must receive as a gift from Him who loves everyone incomprehensibly.

Additional Readings: Romans 11:33-36, 1 Corinthians 2:6-10, 1 Corinthians 13

JANUARY 4

Not that I have already obtained all this, or have already arrived at my goal, but I press on to take hold of that for which Christ Jesus took hold of me. Brothers and sisters, I do not consider myself yet to have taken hold of it. But one thing I do: Forgetting what is behind and straining toward what is ahead, I press on toward the goal to win the prize for which God has called me heavenward in Christ Jesus.
—Philippians 3:12–14

Dear Jesus,

I know that my life isn't quite over because I am still here. I know that, as soon as my body dies, my soul will be perfected. Until I receive that gift, I have a purpose for my life; it's to live out faith and love in your name in an athletic way. It's to press on in ardent, concentrated love toward the day I experience your perfect love and power in heaven. Every now and then, I am overcome by memories of past failures. They turn me inward and downward. But in this passage, Paul tells me that even he willfully forgot what was behind, so he could live fully in the present. Help me today to forget all my sins and failures as well as every supposed accomplishment. These two impostures only distract me from today. Instead, give me the singular purpose to live today the way you have called me to. Thanks for paving the way for me to do this with your pure grace.
AMEN

God has promised to give us grace and forgiveness for the rest of our lives. Let's promise him to run in that sphere with all the spiritual agility we can muster.

Additional Readings: 1 Corinthians 13, 1 Timothy 6:12, Luke 9:62, Hebrews 10:36-39, 1 Corinthians 9:24-27, Romans 8:28-29

JANUARY 5

I want to be found in Christ, not having a righteousness of my own that comes from the law, but that which is through faith in Christ—the righteousness that comes from God on the basis of faith. I want to know Christ—yes, to know the power of his resurrection and participation in his sufferings, becoming like him in his death, and so, somehow, attaining to the resurrection from the dead. –Philippians 3:9–11

Dear God,
You sent your Son to give me what I needed in order to give back to you. I could never be completely right in your eyes. I know what you want. I even nod in approval. But still, I somehow choose to fall short and do my own will each day. Then you, like a mother giving her child the money he needs to buy her a present, give me Jesus to be the righteousness you desire. I believe this, and so I cannot leave your side. Help me to know what it means to live in your Son and to obediently participate in his sufferings. My generation tells me to seek comfort and convenience, but you tell me to seek love and sacrifice. It scares me to think that you have called me to suffer, but I believe it is holy and right to selflessly serve. Now, by your grace, help me experience the sacrificial Christian life with a spiritually mature heart.
AMEN

Jesus came to save us, change us and then make us a replica of him for our generation.

Additional Readings: Romans 3:9-28, Romans 6:23, Romans 8:1-4, Jeremiah 33:14-16

JANUARY 6

But whatever were gains to me I now consider loss for the sake of Christ. What is more, I consider everything a loss because of the surpassing worth of knowing Christ Jesus my Lord, for whose sake I have lost all things. I consider them garbage, that I may gain Christ. —Philippians 3:7-8

Dear Jesus,
I know the story of Paul's life and how you took away all his earthly status and renewed him in the status of grace. He had been so proud of his own accomplishments and then suddenly they meant nothing to him anymore. In the same way, I have already thrown away my childhood trophies, but I struggle to cling to what I consider adult accomplishments. I try not to talk about them, but I still caress them in my thoughts and measure my life by them when I daydream. By your Holy Spirit, I am begging you to free me from the temptation to measure my life by anything other than your grace. Help me to consider even those things I have accomplished as a Christian to be garbage compared to having your unmerited favor. That way, I will be immune to both diseases called success and failure.
AMEN

When Christ fills the room in our hearts, we forget who we were and relax in who we are in him.

Additional Readings: Matthew 13:44-46, Luke 14:33-35, Jeremiah 9:23-24, John 17:3, 2 Peter 1:2-11, Psalm 73

JANUARY 7

For just as each of us has one body, with many members, and these members do not all have the same function, so in Christ we, though many, form one body, and each member belongs to all the others. – Romans 12:4-5

Dear heavenly Father,
You make a very bold statement that I belong to every other Christian and every other Christian belongs to me. We own each other like family. I confess that by nature I like to pick and choose who I want to consider as a brother or sister. I know others can tell it, too. I can tell when they are picking and choosing, also. Lord, forgive us all for being choosy and not submitting to your truth that we are all brothers and sisters who must serve each other in every way. Help me to lead the way by "being there" for others. When I reach my limit and cannot help another Christian that I know needs help, then raise up other Christians to reach out with unconditional love to help that brother or sister in need. Oh, Lord, help us love each other the way you want us to.
AMEN

In Christ there are no "black sheep." All have been made white in the blood of the spotless Lamb who purchased them.

Additional Readings: 1 Corinthians 12:7-26, Ephesians 2:19-22, 1 Peter 4:7-11, Colossians 3:11-12

JANUARY 8

Blessed be the God and Father of our Lord Jesus Christ, who according to His abundant mercy has begotten us again to a living hope through the resurrection of Jesus Christ from the dead, to an inheritance incorruptible and undefiled and that does not fade away, reserved in heaven for you, who are kept by the power of God through faith for salvation ready to be revealed in the last time. –1 Peter 1:3-5

Dear heavenly Father,
By sending Jesus for me you have given me a living hope. He conquered death and gives me the grace and power to live forever after I die. Believing this gives me a sense of optimism even while I am a realist about my situation. My biggest goal is to live joyfully in faith while I love others in your name. Help me be honest with myself about whatever challenges and problems I face, but not depressed by them. I do not have to resolve every problem or achieve every goal when you have promised I will leave them all behind anyway. Oh, Father, make me honest about my earthly life and hopeful in my eternal life at the same time.
AMEN

Real faith honestly treats earthly matters with passing concern and heavenly matters with tenacious respect.

Additional Readings: Luke 12:13-21, 2 Timothy 4:6-8, Mark 8:36

JANUARY 9

By faith Abraham, when called to go to a place he would later receive as his inheritance, obeyed and went, even though he did not know where he was going. – Hebrews 11:8

Dear Jesus,
You would not tell Abraham where he was going but you told him to leave his comfort zone and follow you. Not knowing what that meant for his family and him was exactly what you wanted. You purposefully kept him in the dark. For a long time, I have wondered why you do this to us. I think you don't tell us what is next in our lives so we will stay close to you with an open heart to who you are. You made us to live with you. We tend to live by ourselves, especially when we think we know how things will go for us. Even us Christians are often functional atheists. You held Abraham close, as your friend, by keeping him in the dark. Hold me close to, dear Jesus. I don't know what huge challenges and great opportunities wait for me. I can't figure it out. But I can stay close to you. If you will stay close to me and fill me with the fruits of your Spirit, I will boldly step into an unknown tomorrow. I will go where you lead me. Take the wheel, Jesus. Just don't ever kick me out of your car.
AMEN

God keeps us from knowing what's next in order to keep us close to him now and in the 'what's next'! Having us close to him is why he made us in the first place.

Additional Readings: Genesis 12:1-9, Acts 7:1-8, Hebrews 11

JANUARY 10

If we live, we live for the Lord; and if we die, we die for the Lord. So, whether we live or die, we belong to the Lord. —Romans 14:8

Dear Lord,
Being honest, I would have to admit that all day long I am tempted to measure my happiness by whether I am getting my way or not. I unconsciously ask myself, "Did I get what I want or need?" This verse is a game changer. I belong to you. I was made by you. I was purchased back by you after I got lost. I belong to you. Therefore, I am not master of my own fate or captain of my own ship. This makes me feel safe and secure even if my life in this world is non-descript or even hard. Knowing that I belong to you also binds me to a purpose higher than my own desires. I live for you and I die for you. Help me to live for you as for an audience of One. Restore to me the happiness of a life well lived for the One who lived well for me.
AMEN

Most of our unhappiness is caused by our self-centeredness and self-pity, not by the people or circumstances around us. That's good news because with God's help we can choose to be happy at any moment.

Additional Readings: Philippians 1:12-26, Romans 15:1-13

JANUARY 11

"No," said Peter, "You shall never wash my feet." Jesus answered, "Unless I wash you, you have no part with me. —John 13:8

Dear Jesus,
I understand why Peter's objected to you washing his feet. He adored you. He wanted to honor you, serve you, and keep you on a pedestal. I want to do that too. But glued to my worship of you is also my addiction to myself. It is an uninvited guest that always seems to tag along with my faith in you. That's why you came to wash us, to rescue us. If we do not let you rescue us, we have no part with you. If we are thinking that our worship of you is more important than you, we have subtly and completely missed the point. You are God who loves to save us. We are sinners who must be saved. So, wash away dear Jesus. Wash away my sins and all the sins of my family and friends. Flood our lives and relationships with your cleansing grace and drive out the judgement and selfishness that so easily tears us apart.
AMEN

"It's all about Jesus and his cleansing grace. If he doesn't wash us, we will live dirty selfish lives toward each other."

Additional Readings: Galatians 3:1-14, 5:1-6, Titus 2:11-14, Titus 3:3-8

Donald W. Patterson

JANUARY 12

Jesus said to his disciples: "Take courage! It is I. Don't be afraid." "Lord, if it's you," Peter replied, "tell me to come to you on the water." "Come," he said. Then Peter got down out of the boat, walked on the water and came toward Jesus. But when he saw the wind, he was afraid and, beginning to sink, cried out, "Lord, save me!" Immediately Jesus reached out his hand and caught him. "You of little faith," he said, "why did you doubt?" —Matthew 14:27-31

Dear Jesus,

If it is you who is walking over the waters of my life, then call out to me and ask me to come out there with you. There are several things that make me anxious and I am not sure what to do with them. They are like the wind and the waves that galloped on the night you surprised the disciples. I am so tempted to stare at the problems with fearful eyes and no ideas about what to do. Fix my eyes on you and give me the wisdom and insight to do what you would do, trusting that you will hold me up above the waters that churn to engulf me. Be my Savior in the difficult moments just as you were at the cross.
AMEN

Peter doesn't walk on water anymore. It's our turn to trust and obey.

Additional Readings: Exodus 14:13-14, 2 Chronicles 20:12, Daniel 10:12, Matthew 9:1-8, 17:7, 28:10, Acts 23:11, Revelation 1:17

JANUARY 13

My son, keep your father's command and do not forsake your mother's teaching. Bind them always on your heart; fasten them around your neck. When you walk, they will guide you; when you sleep, they will watch over you; when you awake, they will speak to you. For this command is a lamp, this teaching is a light, and correction and instruction are the way to life. Proverbs 6:20-23

Dear Jesus,

You gave me great parents who labored tirelessly to rear my siblings and me with careful instruction and love. I know their rules, instructions and modeling were all from the faithful heart of parents who owned the success of their children. I grieve even today about the times I made their work stressful or difficult. However, now all their work is bearing fruit long after they have entered your palace in heaven. Help me honor my parents and you by doing from the heart what they engraved there. Encourage parents everywhere that you are proud of them when they invest time, energy and insight in the children you have loaned them. Help them have faith that one day their children will pray like this. Encourage them, so they do not give up in the face of temporary resistance.
AMEN

God invented parents and families. He highly esteems this arrangement. That's why he protects it with one of his "Big Ten" commandments.

Additional Readings: Exodus 20:12, Deuteronomy 6:4-9, Psalm 119:105, Proverbs 3:21-26, 1:7-9, 10:17

JANUARY 14

There is a time for everything, and a season for every activity under the heavens: a time to be born and a time to die, a time to plant and a time to uproot, a time to kill and a time to heal, a time to tear down and a time to build, a time to weep and a time to laugh, a time to mourn and a time to dance, a time to scatter stones and a time to gather them, a time to embrace and a time to refrain from embracing, a time to search and a time to give up, a time to keep and a time to throw away, a time to tear and a time to mend, a time to be silent and a time to speak, a time to love and a time to hate, a time for war and a time for peace. —Ecclesiastes 3:1-8

Dear Lord,

I did not ask to live in this time and place. You placed me here right where you want me. But ever since I got here, I have tried to control time and place. It always sets me up for frustration and makes me lose the joy of the moment no matter what "time" it is. Help me to savor the time you have given while I have it, to use it for good and to do what is appropriate for each "time." Give me wisdom to know when to save and when to toss, when to tear down and when to build up, when to stay put and when to move. Help my family and friends with this same challenge. I cannot stop time from passing, but I can stop just passing through time. I want to worship throughout my entire time on earth and make every second count.

AMEN

Time cannot be created, stopped, saved, or exploited. It runs its course for everyone, and no one can keep it forever. It cannot help or hurt you by itself. In heaven, the anxiety caused by time will be forever forgotten.

Additional Readings: Acts 17:22-31, Ephesians 1:3-23

JANUARY 15

Where there are no oxen, the manger is empty, but from the strength of an ox come abundant harvests. – Proverbs 14:4

Dear Lord,
I know that a neat and tidy home, yard, and office make me more efficient and communicate to you and others that I appreciate everything you have given me. But I also know how neatness can make my possessions become idols that I coddle and protect. I can even make messes of other people's emotions if they make a mess out of my tidy things. Help me to appreciate that a home that is slightly messy is lived in by people I love, that a disheveled desk means I have productive work that makes my life matter, and that a yard that needs mowing is a healthy yard with growing things. Give me enough of life to keep it a little messy and enough thankfulness to take proper care of everything you loan to me. Above all, help me truly value people more than things.
AMEN

The goal is productive, thankful living, not becoming a curator of my own private, tidy museum.

Additional Reading: Psalm 144, Malachi 3:6-12, 2 Corinthians 9:1-12-15

JANUARY 16

We all, like sheep, have gone astray; each of us has turned to our own way; and the Lord has laid on him the iniquity of us all. —Isaiah 53:6

Dear Lord,
If John 3:16 is the gospel in a nutshell, then this passage is the gospel in a matchbox. It is very comforting to be able to admit that I am a sheep that strays every day. It gives me freedom from trying to be perfect in order to feel good about life. Instead, I get to feel good about this; you have laid my iniquity on your Son. Thank you for signing up to be my God and Savior. I realize it cost you everything. I gladly sign up to be your sheep. I will do all I can to receive your grace with a grateful heart and will try to be good to all your other sheep for your glory and their good.
AMEN

When you know who and what you are and stop trying to be something you're not, then you have made a giant stride in spiritual growth.

Additional Reading: Psalm 130, 1 Peter 2:21-25, Romans 4:25 2 Corinthians 5:16-21, Ephesians 4:32

JANUARY 17

The heavens declare the glory of God. The skies show the work of his hands. – Psalm 19:1

Dear Lord,
I see your creativity and amazing power in every sunrise and sunset. They remind me that you are there and that you govern everything happening under them. It gives me peace to know that it is your gracious and forgiving hand that turns the world and paints the sky. I know how little I deserve your blessing, but I also know that I am loved as much as everyone else. I will dedicate myself to loving everyone today in the same way that you paint skies for the evil and the good.
Amen

God loves each of us so much that he counts our hairs every morning and paints us a picture in the skies every night.

Additional Reading: Psalm 50, Psalm 89, Isaiah 40:21-22, Acts 14:14-18, Romans 1:18-20

JANUARY 18

Yet you desired faithfulness even in the womb; you taught me wisdom in that secret place. – Psalm 51:6

Dear Heavenly Father,
You saw my need for your presence to keep me honest and humble even from my mother's womb. You were teaching my heart the difference between truth and error even there. Since then I have had so many voices teach me otherwise. Sometimes, I get confused and cannot tell the difference between right and wrong. But your word is light for my darkened soul. Help me today to be honest enough with myself to consult your word and those who know it well, in order to guide my life into pleasing you. I want to get as close to living like Jesus as I can, not for any prideful reason, but because that will be what is best for the people you have decided would see me today.
AMEN

Why would we work so hard to pretend that we are not all that sinful when Jesus' gospel says that the very reason, he came was to redeem us from a boat load of sins?

Additional Reading: Genesis 6:5-8, 9:12-17, John 4:1-26, Hebrews 4:12-13

JANUARY 19

What causes fights and quarrels among you? Don't they come from your desires that battle within you? You desire but do not have, so you kill. You covet but you cannot get what you want, so you quarrel and fight. You do not have because you do not ask God. When you ask, you do not receive, because you ask with wrong motives, that you may spend what you get on your pleasures. —James 4:1-3

Lord,
Every time I read this passage I want to say, "Really? It's that simple?" But I know it is. I cannot blame any fighting or discontent on all the people around me. I must admit it; I have desires that well up in me and they make me work hard and fast to get them met. But here you correct me. You tell me that praying to you, oh God, ends fighting. It replaces lust with trust and brings you back into every relationship. I know this by experience. When I have prayed for what love or blessing, I want from others instead of fighting for it, you either moved them to give me what I need or you changed my heart to want to serve more than be served. Prayer ends fights. Lord, help me to remember to pray about things that bother me today more than I scheme on how to fix them. Then give me eyes to see when you answer my prayer tenfold.
AMEN

It's not what's happening or not happening outside of us that dictates our peace and joy. It's what is happening or not happening within us.

Additional Reading: Titus 3:3-11, Romans 7:23, Matthew 15:10-20, Ephesians 3:31-32, 1 John 3:15-24

Donald W. Patterson

JANUARY 20

Can any one of you by worrying add a single hour to your life
—Matthew 6:27

Dear Jesus,
With this little sentence you both comfort and confront me. I am comforted that my life does not depend on my own or anyone else's decisions. I am confronted that I waste way too much time worrying as if it does. Help me find the balance between responsible stewardship of my body and life and careless faith that makes me sleep well and not live with stress every day. You had a relatively short life on earth compared to mine and you did not waste one ounce of energy worrying. Come and rescue me from the same.
AMEN

Peace about our future comes when we trust who holds it. Don't strain to see the future. Strain to see who is holding it.

Additional Reading: Psalm 39, Psalm 90, Psalm 104, Acts 17:22-31

JANUARY 21

Be strong and courageous. Do not be afraid or terrified because of them, for your God goes with you; he will never leave you nor forsake you. – Deuteronomy 31:6

Lord,
I love this promise you gave Israel through Moses. It reminds me that all the concerns I have about our country, my church, my finances, my health, and the welfare of my loved ones, every one of them is overwhelmed with this one thought; You are with me. With your power and love right by my side, I cannot give way to fear. I am going to be okay and so will everyone else. You are with me. And even if I die, I will then see you in all your glory instead of only experiencing you through words. Oh God, help me live today with a comforted heart.
AMEN

Finding peace in God frees us to enjoy the blessings of each day.

Additional Reading: Joshua 1:5-11, Matthew 28:18-20, Isaiah 41:17, Hebrews 13:4-8, 2 Chronicles 16:9

JANUARY 22

Let the peace of Christ rule in your hearts, since as members of one body you were called to peace. And be thankful. —Colossians 3:15

Dear Jesus,
I love how the words, "be thankful" just creep into grand passages about peace from our relationship with you. I try to imagine descriptors of you when you walked the earth and I think one would be that you were always thankful. I cannot see you complaining about a messy house or a messy roommate. I cannot see you stressing everyone out by what you cannot get accomplished. I don't think you ever complained when you were small because your mom cut the sandwich into triangles instead of squares. You never complained and always thanked your Father and people genuinely. I on the other hand am a "chronic complainer." I know it even when no one else notices because I complain in my heart. In fact, I complain so much that I get bored by my own complaining. Jesus, make me a thankful person like you. More importantly, thank you for forgiving my ungrateful heart. I want to live a thankful life because you accept me with a gracious heart. When I do live a thankful life, I feel the peace you talk about too.
AMEN

Complaint is really an identity issue. If you see yourself as blessed without merit you will not complain about much. Until God changes how you look at yourself, you won't stop being unhappy with everyone and everything.

Additional Reading: John 14:27, Romans 1:21, Philippians 2:14-18

JANUARY 23

Oh, the depth of the riches of the wisdom and knowledge of God! How unsearchable his judgments, and his paths beyond tracing out! "Who has known the mind of the Lord? Or who has been his counselor?" "Who has ever given to God, that God should repay them?" For from him and through him and for him are all things. To him be the glory forever! Amen. —Romans 11:33-36

Dear Lord,
Thank you for never hiring me to plan and execute the big things in my life. Although, I have doubted you too many times to count; I always like the end you write for each chapter of my life. I do get stuck too often begging for you to show me your ways and your plans before I dare step forward with a willing heart. I am so sorry for being so stubborn. But now I ask, please graciously keep writing my story for Jesus' sake. And don't tell me how it ends. I want to wait until I get there where I will have to hold on tightly to your right hand lest I slip into the unhappy ending that you have prepared for demons and not for people.
AMEN

It's your choice: Either write your own story and force God to write an unhappy ending. Or let God write your story and look forward to an amazing finish.

Additional Reading: Psalm 73, Psalm 139, Esther, Ruth, Ecclesiastes 8:16-17, Ephesians 1:11, Revelation 5

JANUARY 24

Hide your face from my sins and blot out all my iniquity. Create in me a pure heart, O God, and renew a steadfast spirit within me
—Psalm 51:9-10

Lord,
My natal spiritual defect is that I have a corrupted heart. From that heart I have erred in too many ways to count. I know I am forgiven. But what I ask today is that you create a new heart in me for today. Use the new morning mercy you promise to change who I am today. I am dependent on your daily medicine. Oh, God I do not want the placebo that the world offers to cheer my soul. I want the real thing, pure grace. Make me a new, selfless, happy, and generous person today–all because I know I am forgiven and loved by you. Take away my judgmental, unhappy heart and give me the steroid that helps me walk three feet above who I would be today without you.
AMEN

The human soul is the epicenter where grace works. All good human operations come from the changes that happen inside and not outside of that holy room.

Additional Reading: Jeremiah 17:5-10, Genesis 50:20-21, Matthew 5:1-12

JANUARY 25

To some who were confident of their own righteousness and looked down on everyone else, Jesus told this parable: 'Two men went up to the temple to pray, one a Pharisee and the other a tax collector. The Pharisee stood by himself and prayed: 'God, I thank you that I am not like other people — robbers, evildoers, adulterers — or even like this tax collector. I fast twice a week and give a tenth of all I get.' 'But the tax collector stood at a distance. He would not even look up to heaven, but beat his breast and said, 'God, have mercy on me, a sinner.' 'I tell you that this man, rather than the other, went home justified before God. For all those who exalt themselves will be humbled, and those who humble themselves will be exalted. – Luke 18:9-14

Dear Jesus,

With this simple story of a spiritual giant (the tax collector), and a religious dwarf (the Pharisee), you put holy fear in me of becoming self-righteous. I fear because I not only have looked down on people who have repetitive public sins, but I have also looked down on the Pharisee, because I am sure I have not looked down on others as much as he. Oh Jesus, if I am honest with myself, I look down on everyone for one reason or another at different times. I struggle with the damning sin of self-righteousness. Oh, please forgive my sin and purify my heart from thinking I am any different than the rest of fallen humanity. Be my Savior and light the way out of my dark and lonely cave of self-righteousness. Help me to truly esteem all others better than myself.
AMEN

The one sin I am proud to have never committed is the sin of looking down on others, or so I thought!

Additional Reading: Philippians 2:1-11, James 1:27, Jeremiah 31:16-20

Donald W. Patterson

JANUARY 26

Who is wise and understanding among you? Let them show it by their good life, by deeds done in the humility that comes from wisdom. But if you harbor bitter envy and selfish ambition in your hearts, do not boast about it or deny the truth. Such "wisdom" does not come down from heaven but is earthly, unspiritual, demonic. For where you have envy and selfish ambition, there you find disorder and every evil practice. But the wisdom that comes from heaven is first of all pure; then peace-loving, considerate, submissive, full of mercy and good fruit, impartial and sincere. Peacemakers who sow in peace reap a harvest of righteousness. —James 3:13-16

Oh God,
Give me wisdom that is not afraid to ask for help, not too proud of its own opinion, more bent on unity than being right, more concerned about mercy than justice. Give me the kind of wisdom that makes others want to play in the sand box with me for the good of all. Help me to hide my opinion much longer than feels comfortable while I learn to listen to others to try to understand not only their opinion but the context from which they have formed it. Give me the wisdom that comes from love for you and people instead of that so called "wisdom" that comes from pride and ambition. Make me a servant with my experience rather than a blind "know it all."
AMEN

Wisdom from God makes us uniquely love all people, even those that oppose us.

Additional Reading: Philippians 2:1-11, James 1:19-20, 2 Corinthians 12:1-10

JANUARY 27

So then, just as you received Christ Jesus as Lord, continue to live your lives in him, rooted and built up in him, strengthened in the faith as you were taught, and overflowing with thankfulness. —Colossians 2:6-7

Dear Lord,
Almost daily I check to see if my life is "good" by some human measurement. Like, "Is it good because of my financial position?" Or "Is it good because of my position in my work?" Or "Is it good because I have control of my weight?" Or "Is it good because I have my way in key relationships?" Or "Is it good because I have the favor of others?" Or "Is it good because my church is growing and going?" Or "Is it good because I get to live where I want to?" Or "Is it good because the weather is cool and refreshing and sunny?" All these questions leave me empty whether I answer "yes" or "no" to them. My life is good because I have you as my Lord and Savior. I have your love, your promise to be with me, your commitment to work everything for my eternal good, and your guarantee of a home in heaven. Oh Jesus, help me live thankfully in the good life you have given me just by saving me and calling me your own.
AMEN

Jesus promised that he would give us an abundant life along with eternal life. If we don't feel that we are getting the abundant life, we are most likely missing the point.

Additional Reading: Psalm 145, Matthew 11:28-30, Matthew 16:24-27, John 10:1-18, Colossians 1:3-13

JANUARY 28

Rejoice with those who rejoice; mourn with those who mourn. Live in harmony with one another. —Romans 12:14-15

Dear Heavenly Father,
I see in your word that you want me to be an active, interdependent part of the larger body of Christ at my church; but in my heart, there is another force that drives me to keep things on the surface, to only see my church as a place to attend and not a community to bless and be blessed by. Your word above is very clear. The picture of harmonizing shows how closely you want me to be connected to my family of believers so that I rejoice in the good things happening in their lives and I grieve with them when they are grieving. You want me to be caught deeply in the web of Christian relationships. Oh Father, help me to be more vulnerable to the people at my church and give me the opportunity and ability to become more of a close friend to the people there.
AMEN

Being connected to a church family is vastly more than simply attending a Sunday service that we like.

Additional Reading: Matthew 5:43-48, Job 30:25, 1 Corinthians 12:4-27

JANUARY 29

Be careful not to practice your righteousness in front of others to be seen by them. If you do, you will have no reward from your Father in heaven. So when you give to the needy, do not announce it with trumpets, as the hypocrites do in the synagogues and on the streets, to be honored by others. Truly I tell you, they have received their reward in full. But when you give to the needy, do not let your left hand know what your right hand is doing, so that your giving may be in secret. Then your Father, who sees what is done in secret, will reward you. —Matthew 6:1–4

Dear Heavenly Father,
Forgive me for patting myself on the back so often when you move me to do something generous for someone else. And forgive me for telling my family what I have done in order to remind them that I am so good to them. I beg you to free me from the need for affirmation and recognition from any human being. Help me to do ten times more good things for others but to do them in secret before you so that my life reflects your constant unnoticeable love that holds us up every day behind the scenes. I want to be like you, loving freely without needing recognition.
AMEN

Godly generosity has amnesia about what it has done.

Additional Reading: Colossians 3:23-24, 2 Corinthians 9:6-15

JANUARY 30

Nothing can hinder the Lord from saving, whether by many or by few.
—1 Samuel 14:7

Dear Jesus,
You put these words in Jonathan's mouth when he was about to face a whole army of Philistines with only his armor bearer and his sword. With a supernatural faith he firmly trusted in you to deliver him. I want that supernatural faith. All I know to do is to beg for it. I cannot manufacture it in this broken heart of mine. There are too many broken parts. Please give me the faith of Jonathan to trust that you will deliver me in every situation. Free me, dear Lord, of all worry that so easily preoccupies my mind and makes me unfruitful for others. Give me peace that you are holding me and protecting me from my enemies, whether they are health problems, wild gunman, economic challenges or friends turned to critics. I want to trust you with a clear conscience.
AMEN

God helps those who cannot help themselves.

Additional Reading: 1 Samuel 14:1-14, Exodus 14:1-31, Hebrews 13:5-6

JANUARY 31

As for God, his way is perfect: The Lord's word is flawless; he shields all who take refuge in him. – Psalm 18:30

Dear Father in Heaven,
I do not want to keep begging in the same old mundane way, "Lord, please do this or that because I know what I need." Instead, I want to honestly pray, "Thank you for perfectly ordering my life and for leaving behind your word to guide me through the dark forest." I want a trusting, thankful heart, not a heart that always gives you advice. Change me Lord and make me like your Son who trusted you even when you made his life a guilt offering for others.
AMEN

Peace is learning to trust God more than advise him.

Additional Reading: Deuteronomy 32:1-4, Psalm 139, Romans 11:33-36, Revelations 15:3-4, Proverbs 3:5-6, Proverbs 30:1-9.

FEBRUARY 1

Now he who supplies seed to the sower and bread for food will also supply and increase your store of seed and will enlarge the harvest of your righteousness. You will be enriched in every way so that you can be generous on every occasion, and through us your generosity will result in thanksgiving to God. −2 Corinthians 9:10−11

Dear Lord Jesus,
There is a lie that harasses me that goes like this: "If I give too much, I will not have enough for myself." When I hear your promise in the passage above it blows that lie out of the water. I cannot out give you. You will continue to give to me all that I need to have more than enough so I can enjoy being generous all my life. I want to be a powerful giver causing people to be thankful to God by what you move me to give. Oh God, make me a careless giver. Make me care less about myself and more about the needs of others, just like your Son cared less for himself when he gave it all for me.
AMEN

Generosity is acting out of faith that you cannot out give God.

Additional Reading: Isaiah 55:6-13, Proverbs 11:24, Ecclesiastes 11:1-6, Malachi 3:6-12

FEBRUARY 2

Therefore, in order to keep me from becoming conceited, I was given a thorn in my flesh, a messenger of Satan, to torment me. −2 Corinthians 12:7

Dear Lord Jesus,
The Apostle Paul realized that his thorn in his flesh (a physical ailment) was a gift from you to keep him from being conceited. I must confess that I rarely think that my wrinkles and medical problems are a gift from you to keep me from being conceited. But I believe now that you are using them that way for me. My physical problems prove to me that I am fragile and in great need of a God to sustain and deliver me. Everyone else sees that I am weak and needy, but I delude myself into thinking that I am strong and need no help. Frankly, my medical problems make me beg for help because I cannot fix them on my own. Dear Lord, I do not want to be so arrogant as to live as if I do not have any weaknesses or to live like I don't need you who made me. I need you every hour. I need you to help me. Please, give me the self-discipline to take care of my body. Give me the healing I need in order to continue as a servant for you. Bring answers to my unanswered questions. Help me to have the humility to ask for help when I need it.
AMEN

Our problem is not our weakness. It's our delusions of strength that keep us from seeking the grace that strengthens us in our weaknesses.

Additional Reading: Matthew 4:1-5, 1 Corinthians 2, Philippians 4:4-13

FEBRUARY 3

You will keep in perfect peace those whose minds are steadfast, because they trust in you. —Isaiah 26:3

Dear Jesus,
I want to be in perfect peace today. So, pull my chin away from staring at the things that bug me. And make me look squarely at your loving smile that promises that I am loved, forgiven, and that I have you turning what looks like a bad thing into a great thing for my life. I trust you to use those people that I do not trust to make a blessing come to my life. I know that you promise to make every event no matter how big or small, positive or negative, to be part of the grand story of redemption that you are working into my life. Give me the perfect peace you promise, by helping me keep these truths in mind by your Holy Spirit.
AMEN

Jesus can be trusted with your entire life story, even if you must live it out with untrustworthy people.

Additional Reading: Psalm 127, Isaiah 9:2-7, 1 Chronicles 5:20, Romans 8:26-36

FEBRUARY 4

Your eyes saw my unformed body; all the days ordained for me were written in your book before one of them came to be. — Psalm 139:16

Dear Heavenly Father,
It's calming and encouraging to know that this day in my life was ordained by you. This day has meaning, purpose, and hope; because it is the day you wanted me to have right now. Protect me from the temptation to disdain today because it has work, or challenges, or doctor's visits, or tough conversations, or mundane activities. Help me not to define today based on what I see with my eyes or think I see with my heart. Help me to accomplish your goals and not worry if all my goals are realized. Help me to value today as a gift from you, my author and Savior. Open my heart to see some new way to make a blessing for another person today that will last in their lives for years. Help me say the type of things that bless and encourage and enlighten. Give me the ability to chain any stinking thinking to the floor of the deepest room in my heart so it does not get out to hurt or tempt anyone else. I receive today as your gift with a thankful heart and I commit myself to use it to your glory. Finally, I look forward to heaven when you will sift through each day with me, including this one, and will show me the immense value of even the smallest word that occurred today.
AMEN

Every single day of our lives is a very well thought out gift from God. Show him how much you value it by living it thoughtfully, humbly, and lovingly for him.

Additional Reading: Psalm 19, Romans 12, 1 Corinthians 13

FEBRUARY 5

Be kind and compassionate to one another, forgiving each other, just as in Christ God forgave you. Ephesians 4:32

Dear Heavenly Father,
Some people make it so easy for me to be kind and loving toward them. Others make it hard. But you challenge me here in this verse to love, forgive, and show kindness to everyone even the "hard to love" people, because of you and not because of them. It is all a matter of which "BECAUSE" drives me. I am begging you to help me love those who have made life uncomfortable for me, to reach out to those who have stiff armed me, to forgive those who have hurt me even before they dare to apologize. I want to love people indiscriminately BECAUSE you love me that way.
AMEN

Unconditional love is supernatural. You can only get it at one place, from one person. No one else has it to give. It is not for sale. It's free for those who believe that all they must do is ask God for it.

Additional Reading: Matthew 6:9-15, Matthew 18:21-35, 1 Peter 3:1-17, Colossians 3:12-17

FEBRUARY 6

But now listen, Jacob, my servant, Israel, whom I have chosen. This is what the Lord says — he who made you, who formed you in the womb, and who will help you: Do not be afraid, Jacob, my servant, Jeshurun, (the upright one) whom I have chosen. Isaiah 44:1-2

Dear Heavenly Father,
I wish I could say that I always live in the peace of knowing that you are nearby watching over my life with a father's heart. But frankly, I struggle with fear as if I am alone against the world. It shows in how anxious I get in so many situations. Your word shoves the truth of your fatherly presence back into my mind. It calms and reminds me of your ownership, help, and grace. Your word does not ask how many times I have forgotten you or if I want to hear its voice. It just speaks to my childlike heart. "Do not be afraid. I am your God. I will work out your life to a blessed end." Dear Father, I acknowledge your presence here at the beginning of my day. Help me to live in the strength of your presence all day. Guide me to the places and people you want me to touch and make my life more than a selfish earthly pursuit.
AMEN

God is with us every moment even when we forget that we are with him.

Additional Reading: Genesis 16:1-16, Isaiah 41:10, Matthew 28:18-20, 2 Corinthians 4:16-15:1-10

FEBRUARY 7

Because of the Lord's great love we are not consumed, for his compassions never fail. They are new every morning; great is your faithfulness. I say to myself, "The Lord is my portion; therefore, I will wait for him
—Lamentations 3:22-24

Dear Jesus,
It is a great privilege for a sinner to awaken every morning. It means that your mercy is still enveloping our lives. I know how very deeply I have hurt you and yet I do not know the full extent of your disappointment. Your mercy makes it hard to tarry long at the pool of guilt. Instead, it moves me quickly to the living, moving waters of forgiveness. When I jump into your forgiveness river, it carries me swiftly past the guilt of my past. I love jumping in this river to swim for you every morning. Oh, Lord, keep me in the river flowing with your grace.
AMEN

Guilt is a stagnant pond of self-made scum. Grace is a living river that's pure enough for a soul to drink.

Additional Reading: Exodus 34:6-7, Psalm 103, Psalm 130, Hosea 11:9, Malachi 3:6-7, Luke 23:45-49.

FEBRUARY 8

I rejoiced with those who said to me, "Let us go to the house of the Lord.
—Psalm 122:1

Dear Lord,

For many, many, years I thought it was a shallow and confusing encouragement when parents and grandparents hounded their kids and grandkids with the question, "Did you go to church?" But the older I get, the more I see how you do great things for the soul in corporate worship. Too many times to count, I have dragged myself to church grudgingly only to leave ecstatic that I somehow found my way there. What you gave me in the message, the songs, and the prayers purified my soul, comforted my heart, and gave me meaning and purpose that I had lost out there on my own. Now, I'm that parent saying, "Did you go to church?" Oh, God help my children and grandchildren get to your house of worship to have their souls saved and resaved.
AMEN

Corporate worship forces us to storm our minds to take sinful thoughts captive and throw them out into the cold.

Additional Reading: 1 Chronicles 29:10-20, Nehemiah 8, Revelation 7: 9-17

FEBRUARY 9

The Sovereign Lord is my strength; he makes my feet like the feet of a deer, he enables me to tread on the heights. For the director of music. On my stringed instruments. —Habakkuk 3:19

Dear Jesus,
I have seen deer jump this way and that to get up narrow winding mountain paths along cliffs. It is amazing to watch. It is just as amazing to think of all the ways you have brought me through the narrowest escapes. In my car, battling health problems, even at sporting events, you have rescued me from near death experiences. Each time it happens, I think of how you must love me. You will make my feet like that of a deer. It is a very comforting thought. I trust you today, tomorrow, and beyond to protect my life until my job is done here on earth. Thank you for giving me peace the world cannot produce.
AMEN

God never stops looking into our crib to see that we are breathing.

Additional Reading: Deuteronomy 33:26-29, Psalm 46, Psalm 146, I Peter 5:8-11

FEBRUARY 10

I pray that Christ may dwell in your hearts by faith; that you, being rooted and grounded in love, may be able to comprehend with all saints what is the breadth, and length, and depth, and height; And to know the love of Christ, which passes knowledge, that you might be filled with all the fullness of God. —Ephesians 3:17-19

Dear Jesus,
The Apostle Paul prayed that you and your unconditional love would dwell in our hearts and that we would grow more and more to know how pervasive your love really is. Please do this for me and my closest friends and family so we love purely without giving up an inch of the truth. Help me comprehend how full and big your love really is. Help me to view all people through your love. By doing this, we will help others see their need for grace without personally judging them. I will relax in your love whenever we recall the many failures with which we have plagued you. Make your love the driver of my soul.
AMEN

Christ's love is bigger than the universe. No one can begin to exhaust the lessons it will teach him.

Additional Reading: John 13:35, Romans 12, 1 Corinthians 13, 1 John 4:7-21

FEBRUARY 11

So, Christ was sacrificed once to take away the sins of many; and he will appear a second time, not to bear sin, but to bring salvation to those who are waiting for him. —Hebrews 9:28

Dear Jesus,
You must really look forward to the day that you get to come back and take us to glory to be with you. I think of how a man buys an engagement ring and cannot wait to give it to his girl. I look forward to that day, too. We meet in my prayers in the anticipation room. I know I will be rescued from every difficult and frustrating relationship when you come back. So, my today will be filled with hope. In that hope I will step out with an excited smile because I am confidence that you are watching over me.
AMEN

Nothing can separate us from God's loving plans to rescue us from every trouble.

Additional Reading: Matthew 25:31-46, Luke 21:27-28, Philippians 3:20-21, Revelation 7:1-8, Revelation 20:1-5

FEBRUARY 12

I tell you this so that no one may deceive you by fine-sounding arguments. For though I am absent from you in body, I am present with you in spirit and delight to see how disciplined you are and how firm your faith in Christ is. −Colossians 2:4−5

Dear Jesus,
Please give me a discerning heart so that I am not easily duped into thinking and believing ideas that ultimately lead away from you. It is so easy to slip into dead end thinking that leaves me a victim of self-indulgence or self-actualization. You, Jesus, are the fullness of love and truth. Help me to grow in your love and truth so I reflect your love to myself and others.
AMEN

To know Christ more is far better than to know oneself more.

Additional Reading: 1 Corinthians 15:20-28, 2 Corinthians 10:3-8, Galatians 1:6-10, Colossians 2

FEBRUARY 13

May I never boast except in the cross of our Lord Jesus Christ, through which the world has been crucified to me, and I to the world.
—Galatians 6:14

Dear Heavenly Father,
As a husband it is so easy to try to find glory for myself in my wife. As a dad, it is tempting to find glory for me in my children and how well they perform. As an employee, it is easy for me to long for the glory of promotion and raises. As a worker I am tempted to find glory in the work I produce. As an American, I have been "cultured" into believing that my car and my home give me glory. I was made to have glory, only it was always supposed to come from you. You want me to feel glory in being made special by you and in being loved so much that you would save me through your Son. All the other gifts only point to your glory making grace. Your grace makes me glorious. I am special because you thought I was worth creating and then buying me back. Help me to find glory in the thought that you chose me. Give me the strength to get off the spinning wheel of chasing earthly glory. You have made me for heaven. Help me to live for heaven, too.
AMEN

Blessings are a sign that God is there for us. The sign never is the thing. The thing is what the sign points to.

Additional Reading: Romans 12:3-8, Galatians 2:20, Colossians 2:6-15, 1 Peter 2:9-10

FEBRUARY 14

"Marriage should be honored by all and the marriage bed kept pure. God will judge the adulterer and all the sexually immoral."
– Hebrews 13:4

Dear Heavenly Father,
You do not pull any punches when it comes to something so dear to your heart. On this Valentine's Day, I join you and your love for marriage. Please protect the hearts of everyone who is married. Make them love each other with an undying humble acceptance. Help them to listen with their hearts wide open, to forgive before their partner even realizes the wrong they have done, to find creative ways to show support and help. Stamp out loneliness that creeps into a marriage and makes one feel cheated and ruined. Be their strength, their light and the way out of their problems. And for all those who are single, give them soul mates for friends who will fill their waking moments with heartfelt conversations which satisfies the deep longing we all have for relationships. And thank you for promising to one day give us the prize, perfect relationships in heaven with all we know and so many more that we will meet.
AMEN

Marriage is God's invention. Let no one treat it lightly.

Additional Reading: Ephesians 5:21-33

FEBRUARY 15

Are not five sparrows sold for two pennies? Yet not one of them is forgotten by God. Indeed, the very hairs of your head are all numbered. Don't be afraid; you are worth more than many sparrows.
—Luke 12:6-7

Dear Heavenly Father,
It gives me great comfort to know that you remember every sparrow and that I am worth far more to you than any of them. I can face today with all its challenges when I know you are behind me planning to bless me. Since I don't need to worry about myself, help me to seize every moment and make it count for the good of others. I want people to be better for having known me today and not worse. So, help me crucify my selfish desire to be served and make me a servant of all.
AMEN

When you know God chose you to be on his team, you are not anxious about any game you might have to play.

Additional Reading: Joshua 1:7-9, 1 Samuel 14:1-14, Matthew 10:24-33, Matthew 28:18-20

FEBRUARY 16

God said to me, "My grace is sufficient for you, for my power is made perfect in weakness.'" Therefore, I will boast all the more gladly about my weaknesses, so that Christ's power may rest on me.
—2 Corinthians 12:9

Dear Heavenly Father,
Too often I try to be all grown up in my heart. I try to live with independent strength that I can be proud of. I unwittingly think you would be proud of me, too. But here in this passage you teach me that you are proud of me when I know my weakness and reach out for your strong hand to help. Being grown up is not being equal to you. It's living as your child just as I did with the earthly father and mother you gave me. Help me to embrace my weaknesses today and to depend on you for help at every turn. Walk me safely across my "parking lot" where there are "cars" that would otherwise run me over.
AMEN

People who know their need for God are among the most enlightened people on the planet.

Additional Reading: Galatians 2:20, Romans 7-8, Philippians 4:13, 1 Corinthians 2:1-5

FEBRUARY 17

Let them give thanks to the Lord for his unfailing love and his wonderful deeds for mankind, for he satisfies the thirsty and fills the hungry with good things. – Psalm 107:8-9

Dear Jesus,
You have shown love for me by giving me life and salvation, friends that many people long for but never seem to get, family that loves and respects me even though they really, really, know me and my scruples, and work that allows me to have an impact for good in society. Protect me from the insatiable appetite for more that prevents me from finding contentment in what you graciously give. Oh Jesus, give me the secret of contentment by allowing me to want what I have and not have all I want. Be the Savior of my attitude as well as my soul. And then, as a changed person, make me generous like you.
AMEN

Contentment is a God given state of mind that is unaffected by any circumstances.

Additional Reading: Psalm 73, Psalm 100, Matthew 6:25-34, Philippians 4:4-13

FEBRUARY 18

A tranquil heart gives life to the flesh, but envy makes the bones rot.
—Proverbs 14:30

Dear Jesus,
You gave yourself so little of everything on this planet when you were here. You only lived 33 years. You never owned a home or had a wife or children. You had no bank account, no fancy toys, and not much of a vacation ever. And yet, you were the most contented and tranquil person we will ever know. Thank you for not ever giving way to envy. I have all those things you did not afford yourself and I struggle with a continual lust for more. Be my Savior from the power of envy and give me the tranquility that comes from abiding faith in the goodness of your Father. AMEN

Envy will pack her bags and catch the first flight out of your heart when you invite Jesus over for a visit.

Additional Reading: 1 Kings 21 and 22, Proverbs 17:22, Luke 12:13-21, Philippians 4:10-13

FEBRUARY 19

Now Jericho was shut up inside and outside because of the people of Israel. None went out, and none came in. And the Lord said to Joshua, "See, I have given Jericho into your hand, with its king and mighty men of valor. You shall march around the city, all the men of war going around the city once. Thus shall you do for six days. Seven priests shall bear seven trumpets of rams' horns before the ark. On the seventh day you shall march around the city seven times, and the priests shall blow the trumpets. And when they make a long blast with the ram's horn, when you hear the sound of the trumpet, then all the people shall shout with a great shout, and the wall of the city will fall down flat, and the people shall go up, everyone straight before him.
—Joshua 6:1–5

Dear Heavenly Father,
You put Joshua and his people in an impossible situation so that you would be their only deliverer. And, oh, how you delivered them. Help me to remember this story when you put me in difficult places. Help me to remember that you love to be the knight in shining armor for all your children. Help me to pray confidently and to look to heaven expectantly for your fantastic solutions. Give me hope and courage to be gentle and patient with everyone around me when I am facing a scary event. Make me like Joshua because without your help I will sin the way cowards do. Thank you for never cowering from anything I am frightened by.
AMEN

Jesus ain't afraid of nuttin'! And he lives inside of you! Don't forget to let him lead you!

Additional Reading: Exodus 33 and 34, Psalm 46, Mark 4:35-41

FEBRUARY 20

"Though we speak in this way, yet in your case, beloved, we feel sure of better things—things that belong to salvation. For God is not unjust so as to overlook your work and the love that you have shown for his name in serving the saints, as you still do. And we desire each one of you to show the same earnestness to have the full assurance of hope until the end, so that you may not be sluggish, but imitators of those who through faith and patience inherit the promises.
—Hebrews 6:9-10

Dear Lord,
I hear comfort and yet urgency in your words above. First, I am comforted that you look down from heaven and see my struggle to love and serve people for you. You are pleased with any meager fruit produced by faith through me. Secondly, I hear the urgency with which you call me to take my faith life seriously as the most important part of my life. Oh Father, work in me the desire and the power to live a godly life, so my life will be a thank offering to you and your Son. Do not leave me stranded to take on my temptations by myself. I need you every hour to be my strength and my shield.
AMEN

God yells at us because we are his starters not the benchwarmers.

Additional Reading: Joshua 1, Hebrews 10:19-39, Revelation 2:8-11

FEBRUARY 21

Oh, the depth of the riches and wisdom and knowledge of God! How unsearchable are his judgments and how inscrutable his ways!
—Romans 11:33

Dear Lord,
Just when I think I have my life under control, you lift your pinky and change everything for me. Just when I think I can see what you are doing and where you are taking me, I realize I have no idea what is next for me. I know you are behind it all. I just don't know what you have in store for me. I join Paul in saying, your wisdom and judgments are past finding out. Instead, I will sit quietly in the back seat and quit asking, "Are we there yet?" After all, I no longer know exactly where my earthly life is going. If you will be there with me, I will be at home. Thank you for the peace that passes human understanding.
AMEN

We do not know what tomorrow holds. But we know who holds tomorrow.

Additional Readings: Genesis 12-25, Psalm 139, Acts 17:22-34, Revelation 20-22

FEBRUARY 22

The Lord your God is in your midst, a mighty one who will save; he will rejoice over you with gladness; he will quiet you by his love; he will exult over you with loud singing. —Zephaniah 3:17

Dear Heavenly Father,
I know how I gushed over my kids and grandkids when they were little. Even now I can't disconnect from them. As their lives go, so goes my life. It is very comforting for me to know that you feel the same way about me, especially when I read in this verse that you don't just watch me, but you work hard to make my life better. By grace alone you have chosen me as your child, and I feel your love in so many ways. Help me to live in the confidence of knowing I am in your arms and that through your Son you are gaga over me.
AMEN

God loves us more than we could ever imagine. If we can imagine that he loves us at all, we won't be able to stop smiling.

Additional Readings: Isaiah 63:7-19, Luke 12:4-12, Ephesians 3:14-21

FEBRUARY 23

An excellent wife who can find? She is far more precious than jewels. She looks well to the ways of her household and does not eat the bread of idleness. Her children rise up and call her blessed; her husband also, and he praises her. —Proverbs 31:10, 27-28

Dear Lord Jesus,
It is so easy for every one of us married people to take our partner for granted. It is easier to think of what they aren't instead of the blessing that they are. Fill us with thankful hearts so we reflect honor and gratitude in how we speak to and about each other. Help us remember that encouragement and praise work so much better than criticism and manipulation. Make our marriages what you have always intended, a reflection of your relationship with your church, one of holy and unconditional devotion and love.
AMEN

God always intended marriage to be a huge thing in our lives. It's the first big blessing he gave Adam after making him.

Additional Readings: Ruth 3:11, Proverbs 12:4, 18:22, 19:14, 31:10-31, Ephesians 5:21-33

FEBRUARY 24

Remember your leaders, who spoke the word of God to you. Consider the outcome of their way of life and imitate their faith. Jesus Christ is the same yesterday and today and forever. —Hebrews 13:7-8

Jesus,
With so many changes in the world, in my nation's political climate, and in my church and family, it is so easy for me to feel insecure and lost. You have brought to yourself so many people who were significant to me. You have moved so many strong Christian friends away from me, too. In trying to fix my insecure heart, I easily want to "check out" by daydreaming about how things used to be. And yet, you want me to live today secure in your love and truth. You never change. You were my rock in those "good ole days" and you will be my rock now. Help me boldly step out into the future by remembering you are with me and that the leaders you have given and taken away have left a piece of themselves in my heart to guide me.
AMEN

Since Jesus and his promise to re-unite us one day never changes; I can live today in hopeful anticipation.

Additional Readings: Psalm 106, 1 Corinthians 16:15-18, Hebrews 13:7-8

FEBRUARY 25

Each of you must put off falsehood and speak truthfully to your neighbor, for we are all members of one body. –Ephesians 4:25

Dear Lord,
Your grace has freed me from the guilt and shame that come from my sins. You also make me trust that you still love me and will bless my life as a restored child of God. With the strength and confidence that come from grace, make me an honest member of your body, the church. First, help me be honest with myself so I do not live in a "make believe" world about who I really am. Next, make me honest with my family and friends so they really know what they are dealing with when they interact with me. Finally, make me honest with even the most casual stranger so they learn that your gospel is creating real, honest people around them. Help me promote faith and trust in every arena of my life so I help you restore humanity to living in the light of love and truth.
AMEN

Live in truth at all costs. Love without counting the cost!

Additional Readings: Psalm 15, Psalm 51, John 4:21-24, Romans 12:3-21, Ephesians 4:17-32

FEBRUARY 26

Put on then, as God's chosen ones, holy and beloved, compassionate hearts, kindness, humility, meekness, and patience, bearing with one another and, if one has a complaint against another, forgiving each other; as the Lord has forgiven you, so you also must forgive.
—Colossians 3:12-13

Dear Jesus,
Every morning I must decide how I will dress that day. Sometimes it gives me a low level of anxiety because the clothes I thought would fit the day are not clean. I have to settle for something less than I hoped. But I see in this passage that you have filled the closet in my heart with a wardrobe that never gets dirty. It's the virtues that come from your love which your Holy Spirit keeps laundered and hanging in my soul. Help me to dress with this patience, humility, forgiveness, and compassion. So, when others encounter me today, they do not remember what I was wearing on my torso as much as they remember what I wore on my soul. Give me your grace that enables me to dress for loving and truthful living.
AMEN

God has given us all amazing clothes to wear on our hearts. Make sure you change into them throughout the day.

Additional Readings: Philippians 2:3-11, 2 Corinthians 6:3-13, Galatians 5:22-23, Ephesians 6:10-20

FEBRUARY 27

Trust in the Lord with all your heart and lean not on your own understanding. – Proverbs 3:5

Dear Heavenly Father,
This verse is counter to everything I have naturally thought since I was conceived! Since the day I was born, my brain has been collating, evaluating, and mastering the data of the world around me. So often it helps me to do the right thing and be effective in many situations. I have learned to trust my own perception and understanding of big and little situations around me. But I do not naturally trust you and the way you guide my life. I don't naturally trust your promise to turn out everything for my good. I start out every day trying to be in control. That's why in my soul, I rejoice in this little famous verse. It frees me from the burden of trying to figure everything out and it confronts my desire to judge every situation with raw reason. Dear Father, help me trust you today in those matters that overwhelm me and give me the supernatural power and wisdom to be the child that lets you drive.
AMEN

Trusting God makes us a childlike adult, deciding to follow God into selfless sacrifice for others and not scream like a child until we get our way.

Additional Readings: Ecclesiastes 11:1-6, Romans 11:33-36, 1 Corinthians 13, James 4:13-15.

FEBRUARY 28

Be joyful in hope, patient in affliction, faithful in prayer
—Romans 12:12

Dear Lord Jesus,
I have rarely seen so much insight packed into so few words as there are in this three-part challenge from your Apostle Paul. Hope does bring joy for me. Please help me to hope in your promises and not in my circumstances. Becoming impatient when I am troubled is a challenge for me. I appreciate being reminded that you have empowered me to be patient and expect me to put your power to work and settle down. And being faithful in prayer is a gentle breeze blowing away the fog of anxiety that clouds my soul when I forget that I can off load my cares and concerns to you. Give me more hope, more patience, and more interest in prayer. In this way, help me fight the good fight of faith. Thank you for loving and forgiving me through it all.
AMEN

When the rubber meets the road, that's when you see what your spiritual tires are made of. If your tread is wearing thin, go to Jesus for some new tires.

Additional Readings: Matthew 6:25-34, 1 Thessalonians 5:17

FEBRUARY 29

Do not worry, saying, 'What shall we eat?' or 'What shall we drink?' or 'What shall we wear?' For the pagans run after all these things, and your heavenly Father knows that you need them. But seek first his kingdom and his righteousness, and all these things will be given to you as well. Therefore, do not worry about tomorrow, for tomorrow will worry about itself. Each day has enough trouble of its own.
—Matthew 6:32–34

Dear Jesus,
I love these words that you spoke in the Sermon on the Mount. I know you lived them perfectly so when I fail by worrying about my bills or fretting over the loss of some possession, I am comforted that your life covers mine and I am righteous by faith. Then, I am free to practice what you preach here. I can pursue the peace of righteousness as a member of your kingdom instead of anxiously trying to make you work for me in mine. Help me seek your kingdom for me and others today and help me to relax because there is nothing to worry about regarding provisions for me and my family.
AMEN

We cannot choose how long we will live. But by grace we can choose how carefree we will live.

Additional Readings: Matthew 19:28-30, Psalm 37

MARCH 1

Better is open rebuke than hidden love. Wounds from a friend can be trusted, but an enemy multiplies kisses. Perfume and incense bring joy to the heart, and the pleasantness of a friend springs from their heartfelt advice. As iron sharpens iron, so one person sharpens another.
Proverbs 27:6,7,9,17

Dear Heavenly Father,
Just as you have given me Jesus, you have also given me Christian friends who honestly love and serve my best interest. Help me to appreciate their honest meddling in my heart. I do not want to be like a schoolboy playing dodge ball jumping this way and that to avoid penetrating conversation. Make me bold to let my friends affect me. But also, help me to affect them with the same loving, honest, god-pleasing advice. It is so easy to imagine everything is good and nothing should be changed while I live with a blind spot that you sent friends to remove. Give all of us the grace that forgives and makes us vulnerable to one another in that good and holy way.
AMEN

Deep personal friendship is dangerous for our vain ceramic egos.

Additional Readings: Psalm 141:5, Proverbs 20:30, Proverbs 28:23, 2 Corinthians 7:8-13

MARCH 2

And he continued, "You have a fine way of setting aside the commands of God in order to observe your own traditions! For Moses said, 'Honor your father and mother,' and, 'Anyone who curses their father or mother is to be put to death.' But you say that if anyone declares that what might have been used to help their father or mother is Corban (that is, devoted to God)—then you no longer let them do anything for their father or mother. Thus you nullify the word of God by your tradition that you have handed down. And you do many things like that. —Mark 7:9–13

Dear Jesus,
I have so many friends and family that are feeling the heavy burden of grief as their parents' health wanes and the flesh like grass loses its beautiful flower. The challenges of role reversal and life altering decisions leaves them overwhelmed with worry. They want to do the right thing. They want to fight their own selfishness and honor their parents the way you ask us to. But it is no easy task. It is so counter intuitive to tell the ones who have given you your life that they must lose their independence and become more the child than the parent. It is all part of the fallenness of our existence. Help both parents and children to rise-up with love, faith, and hope and to cooperate with each other as they suffer through the last days together. Give them your bright light of forgiveness when they don't get it right and hope for the life beyond when they grieve over the end. Oh, God, help us be your people of love and truth as we struggle through caring for one another.
AMEN

Honor your parents in all circumstances even if it means honoring them with a holy struggle for their own safety of body and soul.

Additional Readings: Exodus 20:12, 21:17, Leviticus 20:9

MARCH 3

"Then I said to you, "Do not be terrified; do not be afraid of them. The Lord your God, who is going before you, will fight for you, as he did for you in Egypt, before your very eyes, and in the wilderness. There you saw how the Lord your God carried you, as a father carries his son, all the way you went until you reached this place." In spite of this, you did not trust in the Lord your God, who went ahead of you on your journey, in fire by night and in a cloud by day, to search out places for you to camp and to show you the way you should go."
— Deuteronomy 1:29-33

Dear Heavenly Father,
This candid discourse from your servant Moses to the children of his peers, who had left Egypt with him, reminds me how easy it is to have you right there helping me and yet still complain and lose trust. They had your miraculous deliverance from Egypt. They had signs of your presence every day and still their challenges in the upcoming "Promised Land" made them cower and complain. I want to learn from their mistakes. I want to be optimistic today in the face of the challenges I am experiencing. Thanks for forgiving me of my recent grumbling. Now, pull my eyes toward you and all the promises you give me that apply to my life and the path you have chosen for me. Make me a positive influence and joyful servant in my family, my church, and my community.
AMEN

Joyful service to God by meeting one's responsibilities without fear and grumbling is the gift of faith from God.

Additional Readings: 1 Thessalonians 1:2-10, Philippians 2:12-17, Jude

MARCH 4

A person's wisdom yields patience; it is to one's glory to overlook an offense — Proverbs 19:11

Dear Heavenly Father,
I sometimes sit and wonder why you do not act more quickly to discipline and punish those who make grave mistakes or commit sins in broad daylight. But I see in this passage that you are practicing the wisdom that you lead me to embrace. You are perfect in your patience. You even let the mistakes of people work a good plan and ultimately help both the sin maker and sin's victim. It is to your glory to overlook my offenses and refrain from nagging me all day long with how I have, yet again, failed you. Now, oh Father, full of love, make me the same kind of wise leader that you are. Help me to exude patience and to overlook the many ways I could be slighted every day. Help me focus on the big things like love, restoration, and encouragement.
AMEN

Eagles do not swat at gnats. Neither should God's people become petty and picky.

Additional Readings: Psalm 130, Proverbs 16:32, Colossians 3:12-14

MARCH 5

Fools find no pleasure in understanding but delight in airing their own opinions. – Proverbs 18:2

Dear Lord,
Give me the grace today to not so much seek to be understood as to understand. Help me to honor the fact that you have given me two ears and one mouth and to trust that I can do more with my ears as I listen with the intent to understand. When I do open my mouth, help me to ask kind and thoughtful questions that reach deeper into the heart of the other person. After I have fully comprehended what they are feeling, thinking, and saying, then help me to answer in such a way that shows humility and love as I give whatever two cents I have left to give.
AMEN

To seek to understand is the first fruit of wisdom.

Additional Readings: James 1:16-27, James 3:12-18

MARCH 6

I pray that you, being rooted and established in Christ love, may have power together with all of God's people to grasp how wide and long and high and deep is the love of Christ and to know this love that surpasses knowledge that you may be filled with the measure of all the fullness of God. —Ephesians 3:17-19

Dear Heavenly Father,
I awakened this morning, as always, with conditions placed on my love for others. Unconsciously, I put them in different classes, some deserving my love more than others. It's like they are on a huge bell curve. I know this is wrong. But without your supernatural, unconditional love working in me, I will be stuck here all day. So, fill me with your love that makes me forget whether I like someone or not. And give me at least one moment today that I consciously choose to love someone that would have been low on my conditional "love scale." Work in me the love that is wider, deeper, and higher than my mind and heart.
Amen

The heart of Christ is to love without discrimination.

Additional Readings: Romans 13:10, 1 John 4 and 5.

MARCH 7

After Jesus and his disciples arrived in Capernaum, the collectors of the two-drachma temple tax came to Peter and asked, "Doesn't your teacher pay the temple tax?" "Yes, he does," he replied. When Peter came into the house, Jesus was the first to speak. "What do you think, Simon?" he asked. "From whom do the kings of the earth collect duty and taxes—from their own children or from others?" "From others," Peter answered. "Then the children are exempt," Jesus said to him. "But so that we may not cause offense, go to the lake and throw out your line. Take the first fish you catch; open its mouth and you will find a four-drachma coin. Take it and give it to them for my tax and yours. —Matthew 17:24-27

Dear Jesus,

I usually think of taxes as something I must pay, but you show me in the same way you showed Peter that you give me what I need to pay my taxes in this world. Since I know you will provide for my tax bill, help me to live free from worry or the begrudging spirit that makes me despise government, so I can be positive and glow with the hope that comes from being in your kingdom. Thank you for the deeply flawed government you have given me as an American. It is my government as a gift from you, warts and all! And finally, if you can pull a coin from a fish for your friend Peter, I trust you can find money from wild places to help me in my needs from now until I step into heaven. So, I will live in peace and freedom.
AMEN

If Jesus will use a fish to give a dollar to a friend, anticipate some wild stories in your own life about his provisions.

Additional Readings: Deuteronomy 8:1-5, Luke 5:1-11, Romans 13:1-7, 2 Corinthians 9:6-15

MARCH 8

He who did not spare his own Son, but gave him up for us all—how will he not also, along with him, graciously give us all things?
—Romans 8:32

Dear Heavenly Father,
Sometimes the hard things in my life make me wonder if you are there or if you have good plans for me. Then I remember this verse and think, "If you gave up your own Son for me, surely you have my best interest at heart. It's just that you haven't brought the "good" to its completion yet. Help me to practice my faith by waiting with sublime faith that you have everything planned for my good, instead of fretting and doubting and making others stressed with words and actions that come from my own anxiety. Give me the strength I need to live above my natural inclinations.
AMEN

God is working everything out for your good whether you enjoy peace from that thought or not. Cash in on the blessing of faith now.

Additional Readings: Genesis 22:1-19, Malachi 3:17-18, Matthew 6:22-34, Romans 8

MARCH 9

Praise be to the God and Father of our Lord Jesus Christ, who has blessed us in the heavenly realms with every spiritual blessing in Christ. For he chose us in him before the creation of the world to be holy and blameless in his sight. In love he predestined us for adoption to sonship through Jesus Christ, in accordance with his pleasure and will — to the praise of his glorious grace, which he has freely given us in the One he loves. —Ephesians 1:3-6

Dear Heavenly Father,
When I read the passage above with my heart wide open, it occurs to me that you are telling a story about me and how you chose me from eternity, saved me in my lifetime and still plan to bless me from now on. You include me in your story because you carry me in your heart even when I am an embarrassment. You love me 1000 times more than my earthly father did. Thank you. Thank you. Thank you. My heart is full of your fatherly love. It amazes me that you are pleased to you in your heart to choose me, of all people, to learn about your Son and believe.
AMEN

When you know your heavenly Dad loves you, you can face anything life has waiting for you.

Additional Readings: Psalm 23, 2 Corinthians 1:3-11, 1 John 3:1-3

MARCH 10

Before the coming of this faith, we were held in custody under the law, locked up until the faith that was to come would be revealed. So the law was our guardian until Christ came that we might be justified by faith. Now that this faith has come, we are no longer under a guardian. —Galatians 3:23-25

Dear Jesus,
It is so easy to see the Christian faith as a set of theological precepts and rules to govern our lives. But what you have done by bursting forth from heaven and living a perfect life for me has rendered all religious rules obsolete for producing righteousness. Your sacrifice has removed my fear of punishment too. Now I live by your love. Your moral commands are now something that free me from myself and give me a way to know that I am pleasing you. All other rules are guides that help me learn to love. They do not threaten or define me. Sometimes I even need to break those man-made rules in order to show love for someone you put in my life. Help me to know the difference between godly love by breaking a man-made rule and simply using my freedom as an excuse to be rebellious. And help me to be a lover of all people because I am a lover of you, oh God.
AMEN

God's love, shown to us in Christ, makes us trust him so much that we want to do what pleases him even when it's hard or unpopular.

Additional Readings: Luke 6:1-11, Romans 13:10, Galatians 5:1-12

MARCH 11

Like newborn babies, crave pure spiritual milk, so that by it you may grow up in your salvation. –1 Peter 2:2

Dear Jesus,
I naturally crave many things, like recreation, financial stability, praise, money, a nice car, and a nice home. I naturally desire to be right or at least to be thought to be right. I naturally desire the affection of others. But I do not naturally seek the pure spiritual milk of your word. Even though I have tasted how wonderful it is to get pure truth, I often grow bored with it. it is hard to admit. I have noticed that when I neglect your word I often regress in my attitude. I get grumpy and petty. My soul seems like it is bogged down in fog. But your moral truth burns off the fog of my generation's confusion about right and wrong. Your grace washes away the gooey guilt of self-righteousness. Once I get back into the word, I feel so much better. Oh Jesus, make me hungry for your word so that I grow up in my salvation without interruption.
Amen

The word of God is spiritual health food. A steady diet makes us strong and resilient when life comes at us fast.

Additional Readings: Psalm 119, John 8:31-32, Colossians 3:12-17, Hebrews 4:12-13

MARCH 12

Whoever would foster love will cover over an offense. But whoever repeats the matter will separate close friends. Proverbs 17:9

Dear Lord Jesus,
I want to be that guy who fosters love not only between others and me but between all people and their friends. This passage makes me think before I tell anyone about someone else's mistakes. Help me to leave the sins and mistakes of others unmentioned so they are not left lonely as others think negatively about them because of my gossip. Put a guard over my mouth and a peace in my soul as I encourage grace and loyalty between friends and family.
Amen

Love delights to see other people grow in their friendship with one another.

Additional Readings: 2 Samuel 15, James 3

MARCH 13

"In everything I did, I showed you that by this kind of hard work we must help the weak, remembering the words the Lord Jesus himself said: 'It is more blessed to give than to receive.'" –Acts 20:35

Dear Jesus,
These words that the Apostle Paul spoke to the elders from Ephesus, before he left them for the last time, give me "core values" for my day. Help me to find joy in the hard work that helps people who need my help. Stop me from stressing myself out by constantly counting how much I have done and how much I have yet to do. Instead, help me be joyful that you have made my life so full that I can work hard with significant purpose in every moment. Also, help me to turn off time wasting screens (phone, computer, TV, etc.). I want to go out and live my own reality instead of only observing the "reality" of others. You worked hard for me so I could happily lose myself in working hard for others. Help me live in that happiness.
Amen

Hard work for the benefit of God's greatest creation (people) is never wasted.

Additional Readings: Proverbs 24:27, Proverbs 24:30, 2 Thessalonians 3:6-15

MARCH 14

For we did not follow cleverly devised stories when we told you about the coming of our Lord Jesus Christ in power, but we were eyewitnesses of his majesty. He received honor and glory from God the Father when the voice came to him from the Majestic Glory, saying, "This is my Son, whom I love; with him I am well pleased." We ourselves heard this voice that came from heaven when we were with him on the sacred mountain. —2 Peter 1:16–18

Dear Jesus,
As a leader of people and a public speaker, I know how easy it is to build my teaching around any story that comes along. The story about your life is not something that was made up or refashioned every time an apostle spoke or wrote. It is all bona fide history that demands a response. You came as the only Son of God and humanity's only hope of forgiveness and eternal life. You came to be trusted, followed, and proclaimed. Someday, every one of us will pass before your throne to be judged. This was Peter's point when he said he saw your majesty when you were transfigured before him. You are the only God and he knew it. So, right before he died, he pressed us to learn that his teachings were based on truth and not perception. Help me live today as if your word is the truth and not just one group's suggestions.
AMEN

The truth about Jesus is the concrete foundation under every day of a Christian's life.

Additional Readings: Psalm 25, John 4:1-26, John 18:33-38

MARCH 15

While they were eating, Jesus took bread, and when he had given thanks, he broke it and gave it to his disciples, saying, "Take and eat; this is my body." Then he took a cup, and when he had given thanks, he gave it to them, saying, "Drink from it, all of you. This is my blood of the covenant, which is poured out for many for the forgiveness of sins. I tell you, I will not drink from this fruit of the vine from now on until that day when I drink it new with you in my Father's kingdom." —Matthew 26:26-29

"A new command I give you: Love one another. As I have loved you, so you must love one another. By this everyone will know that you are my disciples, if you love one another." —John 13:34-35

Dear Jesus,
You are love personified and, on the night before you died, you gave us two commands (mandates) that are natural desires for anyone changed by your love. The first was that we would draw near to you often in the Lord's Supper for a hug from heaven from you as we take your very body and blood shed for us. The second is that we love one another as you have loved us. Both mandates given on Maundy Thursday are a delight for my redeemed soul. I love drawing near to you and I love forgiving and loving those around me, both friend and foe. Please deepen my understanding of how the Lord's Supper and the command to love are foundations for my life. Give me insight into how I can reflect what you are teaching me to others in a simple and powerful way too.
AMEN

Additional Readings: Matthew 26, John 13-17

The Lord's Supper is the closest we get to heaven before we pass from this life to the next.

MARCH 16

Who has believed our message and to whom has the arm of the Lord been revealed? ... Surely he took up our pain and bore our suffering, yet we considered him punished by God, stricken by him, and afflicted. But he was pierced for our transgressions, he was crushed for our iniquities; the punishment that brought us peace was on him, and by his wounds we are healed. We all, like sheep, have gone astray, each of us has turned to our own way; and the Lord has laid on him the iniquity of us all. —Isaiah 53: 1, 4-6

Dear Jesus,
I love to meditate on your six hours on the cross for me. When I read these words from Isaiah that were written 600 years before you were born, I realize that, as the eternal God, your heart and soul has always been on the cross. You are always there suffering, always risen, always sending the Holy Spirit, always loving me. Thank you for taking away the thousand plus ways I have disappointed you. Help me to let that same grace flow through me to those who have let me down. I want to live in the shadow of the cross being forgiven and learning to forgive everyone.
AMEN

Grace for me means grace through me. Grace through me means grace from me to others.

Additional Readings: Psalm 2, Psalm 22, Psalm 69, Isaiah 53, Luke 23, Galatians 3:1-14

MARCH 17

As evening approached, there came a rich man from Arimathea, named Joseph, who had himself become a disciple of Jesus. Going to Pilate, he asked for Jesus' body, and Pilate ordered that it be given to him. Joseph took the body, wrapped it in a clean linen cloth, and placed it in his own new tomb that he had cut out of the rock. He rolled a big stone in front of the entrance to the tomb and went away. Mary Magdalene and the other Mary were sitting there opposite the tomb.
—Matthew 27:57-61

Dear Jesus,
Your friends and faithful followers respected your body and placed it in their own space. Their hearts were breaking. Now here we are 2000 years later respecting your resurrection. We celebrate it with special services on the day commemorating the day that you burst open the tomb and restored hope and joy to all humanity. No matter what our disappointments in life, no matter what our medical prognosis, your resurrection gives us hope and joy. Help your Christians everywhere to live in Easter joy no matter what is going on in their lives. Shield them from the heat of day in the shadow of your cross and heat up their cold winter nights with the sunshine from your empty tomb.
AMEN

It is through the foolishness of preaching Christ crucified and arisen that people are rescued for eternity.

Additional Readings: Matthew 27:62-66, 28:1-10, 1 Corinthians 1:18-31

MARCH 18

The heavenly Father said to me, "You are my servant, Israel, in whom I will display my splendor." But I said, "I have labored in vain; I have spent my strength for nothing at all. Yet what is due me is in the Lord's hand, and my reward is with my God." And now the Lord says — he who formed me in the womb to be his servant to bring Jacob back to him and gather Israel to himself, for I am honored in the eyes of the Lord and my God has been my strength — he says: "It is too small a thing for you to be my servant to restore the tribes of Jacob and bring back those of Israel I have kept. I will also make you a light for the Gentiles, that my salvation may reach to the ends of the earth." —Isaiah 49:3-6

Dear Jesus,
You sat outside Jerusalem and deeply contemplated what was about to happen to you. Your life was in your own hands. You could slip away quietly to Galilee and avoid being betrayed, tortured, and crucified. But you ran toward the trouble instead of away from it. You contemplated your prize, my very soul, and you waited anxiously to sacrifice yourself to save me. Help me to contemplate your great work of love today and to spend less time doing and more time thinking deeply about you and your deep commitment to save me. I'm tired of doing. I want to be more than I do. Come and be the Savior of my soul and captivate my thoughts. While I must do many things throughout this day, help me to be in that other place where you were, thinking deeply about your cross.
AMEN

Jesus' entire person is engaged for us. Our worthy response is to be engaged as much as possible for him.

Additional Readings: Isaiah 50:4-9, Luke 9:43-51 Hebrews 12:1-3

MARCH 19

Jesus sat down opposite the place where the offerings were put and watched the crowd putting their money into the temple treasury. Many rich people threw in large amounts. But a poor widow came and put in two very small copper coins, worth only a few cents. Calling his disciples to him, Jesus said, "Truly I tell you, this poor widow has put more into the treasury than all the others. They all gave out of their wealth; but she, out of her poverty, put in everything — all she had to live on. —Mark 12:41-44

Dear Jesus,
You and the widow confront my selfish heart on Tuesday of your last week. She gave all she had to your Father on a Tuesday. You were going to give all you had to your Father on the following Friday. I so easily get proud of my meager gifts. Yet I invariably leave for myself more than I give to you. None of my gifts have equaled your gift of your whole life for mine. Teach me deep in my soul to freely let go of everything I hold dear for the love of your Father and my fellow humankind. I lose only what I try to keep. I know you have secured my place in your heart by your generosity. You love those you have given to. I am thankful to be one of them.
AMEN

Gifts are not measured by the decimals and commas between their numbers but by the beliefs and feelings in the heart that moved the hand to give."

Additional Readings: 1 Chronicles 29, John 12:1-11

Donald W. Patterson

MARCH 20

Jesus entered the temple courts and drove out all who were buying and selling there. He overturned the tables of the money changers and the benches of those selling doves. "It is written," he said to them, 'My house will be called a house of prayer,' but you are making it 'a den of robbers.'" —Matthew 21:12-13

Dear Jesus,
You had zeal for the temple on the last Monday you would be on earth. You had a deep desire that all people would know their Creator and the love he had for them. The temple was supposed to be the place where anyone could find God. And it had become a market where people worked hard to make a living and sometimes by unscrupulous practices. How your shepherd's heart must have burned to see your father's house exploited for mercantile? Your zeal to clean house also started the ball rolling for the men you confronted to plan your execution. You knew that would be the result. Yet, you did it anyway. How deep your love is that you would be the star player in the game that would kill you. All this was for me and my peace of conscience and eternal destiny under grace. I will purpose to think often and deeply about how you spent your last week for me. It makes my love for you grow and gives me a higher purpose to live.
AMEN

God wants all people to be saved. So, when he moves to defend the ministry of his word, everyone better get out of his way.

Additional Readings: Psalm 19, Psalm 139:19-24, Isaiah 56:1-8, Hebrews 12:18-29

MARCH 21

As a prisoner for the Lord, then, I urge you to live a life worthy of the calling you have received. Be completely humble and gentle; be patient, bearing with one another in love. ... Speak the truth in love, and we will grow to become in every respect the mature body of him who is the head, that is, Christ. —Ephesians 4:1-2, 15

Dear Jesus,
I have so many people to talk to every day. Some conversations are casual and entertaining, but others are critical as we problem solve together and work at life as a family, as a church, or as a community. While I am conversing, give me the wisdom, humility, and strength to be gentle, humble, truthful, and full of love. In this way, when I talk to others, I will not be hurting them or hiding behind self-righteousness or selfish ambition. Give me the moment by moment insight I need to treat everyone with the same respect and love that I want from them when they speak to me. And when they are acting inappropriately, give me a grace-oriented love that refuses to be harsh and cold toward them, but rather firm and loving at the same time. I am starting today forgiving everyone. Help me to finish today the same way.
AMEN

The love of Christ at work within us elevates every relationship we have making it holy in the sight of God.

Additional Readings: Colossians 4:2-6, 1 Thessalonians 2:7-12

MARCH 22

Then Mary took about a pint of pure nard, an expensive perfume, she poured it on Jesus feet and wiped his feet with her hair. And the house was filled with the fragrance of the perfume. —John 12:3

Dear Jesus,
I sometimes wonder if you were with me in person would my worship and adoration of you be as obvious as Mary's. She couldn't care less who saw her spend a year's wages on an afternoon of fragrant worship. How deeply she appreciated your impending death for her that she anointed your body for your burial while you were still alive and humbly wiped you with her hair. Like her I know you absorbed the wrath of justice for me, too. I am loved and I am eternal because you lived and died for me. I worship you in my heart. Help me to unashamedly worship you in the presence of others today.
Amen.

When you really love someone, it cannot be hidden from them or anyone else.

Additional Readings: Romans 12:1-3, Hebrews 13:9-13

MARCH 23

Therefore, he is able to save completely those who come to God through him. Because he always lives to intercede for them. —Hebrews 7:25

Dear Jesus,
It is very comforting for me to know that while I am praying to you, you are praying to the Father for me. Your heart is always turned toward me, even when I fail. Also, I can face the uncertainty that this day brings because I know you have covered it with your prayers. With confidence, I face the challenges of today because I know that you, the Father and the Holy Spirit are right here with me. Together we make a "Dream Team". Amen.

Angels rejoice when we come home to God. The Holy Spirit and the Son pray to the Father for us. Our welfare is a family affair in in heaven.

Additional Readings: Romans 8:31-39

MARCH 24

Trust in the Lord with all your heart and lean not on your own understanding. In all your ways acknowledge him and he will direct your path. – Proverbs 3:5-6

Dear Lord,
There are circumstances at my work, in my family, and in my life that I just can't understand. When I think I have it figured out, it seems I get it all wrong and make things more complicated. That's why I love this passage. You tell me to trust that you will work it out and not to depend on my own understanding. So, today I am taking a personal leave of absence from worrying about anything. You get it all. I'll ride in the back seat and enjoy the scenery.
Amen

Trusting God to do his job is our life and our peace.

Additional Readings: Hebrews 11

MARCH 25

Jesus returned to his disciples and found them sleeping and he said to Peter, "Could you not watch with me for one hour. Watch and pray so that you do not fall into temptation. The spirit is willing but the flesh is weak." — Matthew 26:40–41

Dear Jesus,
It was your greatest hour of need and your disciples did not understand how important it was for them to be awake for you and for themselves. I don't think I would have done any better that day because my spirit is willing, but my flesh is weak also. Today, come and strengthen me with your word and your presence so that I watch, pray, and do not fall into any kind of temptation. Thank you for never falling into temptation. My peace is in your righteousness not mine.
Amen

Jesus is always there for us even when we are not completely there for him.

Additional Readings: James 1:13-18, Hebrews 10:19-31

MARCH 26

"Do not let your hearts be troubled. You believe in God; believe also in me. My Father's house has many rooms; if that were not so, would I have told you that I am going there to prepare a place for you? And if I go and prepare a place for you, I will come back and take you to be with me that you also may be where I am." – John 14:1-3

Dear Jesus,
How amazingly thoughtful of you to comfort our hearts on the night before you would be tortured and die. I trust you. I think of how awesome it will be to live in your Father's house with you and all the saints. I wonder what it is like there for my loved ones who have crossed over to glory. Just thinking about all this fills up my emotional cup. I have a place waiting for me near them. What impact can any earthly sorrow have when it all ends with me living forever with you and them? I will spend today as an optimist. Your promise is worthy of my plan to make it a good day.
AMEN

We can smile like a great lotto winner today. In Christ we have hit the jackpot!

Additional Readings: Isaiah 12:1-5, 2 Corinthians 1:3-11

MARCH 27

One of the criminals who hung there hurled insults at him: "Aren't you the Messiah? Save yourself and us!" But the other criminal rebuked him. "Don't you fear God," he said, "since you are under the same sentence? We are punished justly, for we are getting what our deeds deserve. But this man has done nothing wrong." Then he said, "Jesus, remember me when you come into your kingdom." Jesus answered him, "Truly I tell you, today you will be with me in paradise." —Luke 23:39-43

Dear Jesus,
In your three-year ministry you said, "The first will be last and the last will be first." What deep spiritual joy it must have given you during your greatest moment of darkness to announce grace and heaven to the man dying next to you. He was the last whom we would expect to receive your promise and you made him the first to receive heaven through the cross! I think to myself, "If there is room for him, there is room for me." (Pause for reflection.) It is ironic that one dying man would give another dying man eternal life. Help me to live in the same irony; to give life eternal to others who are dying while I myself am on the same dying road. Free me from my addiction to create a heaven on earth that I cannot keep in order to grasp the heaven in glory that cannot be lost. These two things I ask; help me make life on earth better for others and help me give them the better life in heaven by introducing them to you.
AMEN

Jesus gives us two great blessings: 1) The secrets to happiness in a broken world and 2) the secret passage to a world that cannot be broken.

Additional Readings: John 14:1-6, John 18:28-31

MARCH 28

Therefore, as God's chosen people, holy and dearly loved, clothe yourselves with compassion, kindness, humility, gentleness, and patience. Bear with each other and forgive one another if any of you has a grievance against someone. Forgive as the Lord forgave you. And over all these virtues put on love, which binds them all together in perfect unity. —Colossians 3:12-14

Dear Jesus,
I awoke this morning to the list in my mind of everything that needs to be done today and it is so easy to focus on these tasks rather than on virtue. Then I saw your word that makes my heart and life its own personal project. Today, I will dress my heart with you and all the kindness and love that you bring. Help me to value the lives of all other people today more than my own, so I think of ways to fill up their hearts with encouragement and joy by how I treat them.
AMEN

We tend to care deeply about how we look. God tends to care deeply about how we live.

Additional Readings: Psalm 15, Romans 15:1-4, Philippians 2:1-13

MARCH 29

"The thief comes only to steal, kill, and destroy. I have come that they may have life and have it to the full." –John 10:10

Dear Jesus,
My life is full of hope, peace, and love because you have made me your own. Whenever I try to find my meaning and purpose in the passing pleasures of this world it always seems like the "good life" is coming or going but never sticking around for me. But with you in my life I have a contentment that makes me relax and think of others and how I can bless them. My life is full of you, full of love, and full of people. Thank you for keeping me rich!
Amen

Only our souls will survive this present struggle. Our bodies will not. So, true wealth is only what redeems and sustains the soul.

Additional Readings: Psalm 73, Psalm 121, Psalm 139, Jeremiah 17:5-11, Matthew 16:25-27

MARCH 30

Peter went with them, and when he arrived he was taken upstairs to the room (where Dorcas' body was). All the widows stood around him, crying and showing him the robes and other clothing that Dorcas had made while she was still with them. —Acts 9:39

Dear Jesus,
When a loved one passes, we remember the blessings they brought to others. We even minimize their weaknesses. It's strange how families and friends seem to cope better with our weaknesses after we are gone. But it is a testimony of how your grace makes it easy to not count people's sins against them. These widows in the passage above said nothing to Peter about Dorcas' weaknesses. In their grief, they marveled at the blessings she had created. Give my family and friends the freedom to forget the weaknesses of their loved ones who have gone to glory and comfort them with the reminder that you blessed their lives with that loved one and will keep blessing it with others.
Amen

Every person is a blessing to others. We just need the grace to see and enjoy what those blessings are.

Additional Readings: Daniel 12:1-3, Philippians 1:18-26, Revelation 14:13

MARCH 31

"I have brought you glory on earth by finishing the work you gave me to do. And now, Father, glorify me in your presence with the glory I had with you before the world began." —John 17:4-5

Dear Jesus,
I love seeing you pray these words because I have so much unfinished business and so many unchangeable mistakes and sins from the past. You finished everything well for our Father in my place. You are the best big brother that anyone could ever hope to have. You did everything needed to keep me in your family. Since I am a deeply loved child of God through faith in you, I will do everything I can to extend mercy to people around me just as you do. Without worry over what I do not finish, I will do my best to finish the right things with my remaining days and strength.
Amen

Every moment of Jesus' life was lived for you and not himself. Show him how grateful you are by returning the favor.

Additional Readings: Esther 4:12-16, Romans 14:7-9, Romans 1:1-3, Galatians 2:19-21

APRIL 1

So then, just as you received Christ Jesus as Lord, continue to live your lives in him, rooted and built up in him, strengthened in the faith as you were taught, and overflowing with thankfulness.
—Colossians 2:6-7

Dear Jesus,

I remember several times in my life when all the complexities of the human condition were blown away and it seemed that there was only you and me standing together. Each time this happened, it was an overwhelming experience of peace and purity. I left each experience with renewed strength to face anything that came my way because I was fully aware that I was rooted in you. It made me feel strong. I want to live my life in you. It is the secret to my spirituality. It is the true Christian faith. So, today, I ask you again, please remind me of your presence, renew me in your words, strengthen my soul to live by your grace. Otherwise, I will be blown away when the storms life come my way.
Amen

We are no match for the challenges of earthly life without Christ. We must build our lives on Christ and his word in order to whether the storms.

Additional Readings: Matthew 7:24-29, 1 Corinthians 3:10-15, Ephesians 2:19-22, 1 Peter 2:4-10, 2 Peter 1:3-11

APRIL 2

One thing I do: Forgetting what is behind and straining toward what is ahead, I press on toward the goal to win the prize for which God has called me heavenward in Christ Jesus. —Philippians 3:13-14

Dear Jesus,
Sometimes I think that Satan, that great accuser, should be called the god of the past. How quickly a quiet moment of reflection on great moments in my life can be interrupted with reminders of mistakes and moral failures. It's like he is the big memory spoiler. I need help remembering that you have redeemed me from the past. Every one of those sins has been forgiven and, in your presence, I have peace about the past. Now I am free to look forward to the rest of my life with purpose. So, Jesus keep my eyes on the present and future opportunity to love you and people with all my heart. Keep me from looking over my shoulder in guilt or shame. Turn my head in freedom toward the wonderful challenge to live a God-pleasing life. I want to run my race not to overcome my past or my neighbor but to overcome myself with your redeeming grace.
Amen

If Jesus really did for me what he says he did, then I have all I need to live in peace with purpose.

Additional Readings: 1 Corinthians 9:19-23, 2 Corinthians 5:11-21

APRIL 3

"Be merciful, just as your Father is merciful." —Luke 6:36

Lord,
If it were not for your mercies that are new every morning my life would be over. I depend on your mercy to remove my guilt and shame and give me a respectable identity when I stand in front of the mirror or lay my head on my pillow after another fallible day, or when I bear the accurate criticism of others. Why do I not always think to extend that same mercy to those around me? Instead, I am tempted to pick and choose those whom I will forgive. I am a choosy forgiver and I live among people who are choosy forgivers too. I have two requests: 1) Give me your supernatural mercy for my lack of mercy and 2) Make me merciful to everyone else I know or meet. By your grace, I will mentally burn the note cards in my mind that I have on people who have hurt me. Today starts with a clean record for me and everyone else.
Amen

What would it be like if we all rushed to find mercy the way people rushed to find gold?

Additional Readings: Matthew 5:48, Matthew 18:21-35, Ephesians 4:31-32, 1 John 1:5-10, 1 John 4:7-21

APRIL 4

While Jesus was in Bethany, in the home of Simon the Leper, a woman came to him with an alabaster jar of very expensive perfume, which she poured on his head as he was reclining at the table. ... Jesus said, "When she poured this perfume on my body, she did it to prepare me for burial. Truly, I tell you, wherever this gospel is preached throughout the world, what she has done will also be told, in memory of her."
—Matthew 26:6-13

Dear Jesus,

What an amazing inner connection you and Mary must have had. She heard and understood that you were going to willingly exchange your life for hers, so that she could survive death forever. How small her own gift must have seemed compared to yours. She gave a year's worth of wages of perfume. You gave up your entire being. I marvel at her gift and the faith that made her give it. But I marvel ten times more at the gift that you were giving for her and me. Take my life and let it be an alabaster flask for thee. This story causes me to ask myself, "What can I give that shows I understand and appreciate how much you have given me?" I will start by giving you my heart and my obedience today.
Amen

The only way to truly know Jesus, is to know the magnitude of his gift for you.

Additional Readings: Psalm 51:10-17, Romans 12

APRIL 5

And God said, "Let there be lights in the firmament of the heaven to divide the day from the night; and let them be for signs, and for seasons, and for days, and years." –Genesis 1:4

Dear Heavenly Father,
There is grace in the orderly calendar you have established for all humankind. Friends and enemies alike count the same days, weeks, months and years. The biological clocks in animals revolve around the same four seasons. Plants react to your variance of light and dark in predictable annual patterns. Our lives make more sense because we can add year upon year and celebrate anniversaries. Thank you for the gift of time and the stars that help us mark time for our own benefits. They are another testimony to your sustaining grace in and around our lives. Amen

Every day of his created universe is its own unique gift from a generous Creator and Redeemer. Like snowflakes, each day is to be appreciated for its own beauty.

Additional Readings: Psalm 90, Psalm 139, Ecclesiastes 3:1-22, Isaiah 40:27-31

APRIL 6

Immediately Jesus made his disciples get into the boat and go on ahead of him to Bethsaida, while he dismissed the crowd. After leaving them, he went up on a mountainside to pray. Later that night, the boat was in the middle of the lake, and he was alone on land. He saw the disciples straining at the oars, because the wind was against them. Shortly before dawn he went out to them, walking on the lake. He was about to pass by them, but when they saw him walking on the lake, they thought he was a ghost. They cried out, because they all saw him and were terrified. Immediately he spoke to them and said, "Take courage! It is I. Don't be afraid." Then he climbed into the boat with them, and the wind died down. They were completely amazed, for they had not understood about the loaves; their hearts were hardened. –Mark 6:45-52

Lord Jesus,

I see that after miraculously feeding over 5,000 people right before your disciples' eyes, you made them get into a boat that would be tossed about in a terrible storm. For years I didn't see why you did this, but now I do. Their hearts were hardened and would not let go of thinking that everything depended on them. So, you cracked their hearts to break them open and find the child within who would trust that you are always with us and will be our living, loving God in every trial. Now I see a reason why you would make me ride in a life tossed around by unexpected struggle and tragedy. You are breaking the hard shell on distrusting heart. Oh Jesus, come get into my boat and calm the child within me even before you calm the storm. Help me trust you Lord Jesus. I believe some. But I want to believe a lot! I want to be so confident in your presence that I can share the comfort it brings with others, not just from your book or from my head, but from my heart. Amen

In trials remember that God is changing everything you think about him, yourself your life.

Additional Readings: Proverbs 3:5-6, Matthew 6:25-34, Mark 8:14-21

Donald W. Patterson

APRIL 7

When Jesus had finished saying all these things, he said to his disciples, "As you know, the Passover is two days away — and the Son of Man will be handed over to be crucified." Then the chief priests and the elders of the people assembled in the palace of the high priest, whose name was Caiaphas, and they schemed to arrest Jesus secretly and kill him. "But not during the festival," they said, "or there may be a riot among the people." –Matthew 26:1-5

Lord Jesus,
I see the irony in these verses. While you were planning to give the greatest gift for me as the defect-less Lamb of God during the great feast of deliverance, evil men were plotting to take your life. However, they hoped to avoid that feast so as not to cause a riot! Your gift happened when and where you wanted it to. The riot you caused in humanity has dwarfed the one that they feared in Israel. What perfect love! What perfect plan, to die by and for one's enemies all at the same time. I was killed and raised to life in the riot you have caused. And now I live with peace and forgiveness to share with a lonely and selfish race. Help me freely give of myself to stamp out loneliness among sinners as you have freely given to liberate me from my solitary confinement caused by guilt and shame.
Amen

Jesus died to set the world ablaze with a message than cannot be smothered until it has touched every soul with the truth about God's burning love for all human stubble.

Additional Readings: John 12:20-36, Revelation 5

APRIL 8

Whoever says, "I know God," but does not do what he commands is a liar, and the truth is not in that person. But if anyone obeys his word, love for God is truly made complete in them. This is how we know we are in him: Whoever claims to live in him must live as Jesus did.
—1 John 2:4-6

Dear Jesus,
I don't want to be the liar that you expose in this passage, that is; someone who says, "I know God, but I don't need to follow his will." I know you and your love. And I love you. I want to live a peaceful, loving life like you did. I want to love God the Father so much that I resist all peer pressure to conform to the impurities of this world. I want to be honest, fair, and generous toward everyone. But as much as I want to keep every command, evil is right there with me. I still stumble into selfish thoughts and desires. So, be my strength and shield. Even when I fall, make your renewed grace the reason I get it right the next time.
Amen

Two indelible marks of Christian faith are: A) honesty about one's sins and B) a determination to fight those sins with God's help.

Additional Readings: James 1:19-27, 1 John 3

APRIL 9

Those who plan what is good find love and faithfulness. – Proverbs 14:22

Dear Jesus,
From eternity you planned the greatest good and because of that you have found love and faithfulness in the hearts of your people. This is a great core value for me to follow. I will look at all my plans for my day, week, and life and ask, "Is this a plan to bring good to others and glory to God?" Then I will quietly trust that what will come in return from the people I touch is love and faithfulness. I know it won't be perfectly given back to me. But it will be there. There will be good will and loyalty in the hearts of those I serve selflessly. It's because your love and grace work! Because I believe this, I will set my heart on being a conduit of your good will for humanity. Give me long suffering and endurance to love others consistently even when they do immediately give me love in return.
Amen

You can forget a face or a name. But you can never forget being loved.

Additional Readings: Psalm 34, 2 Corinthians 9

APRIL 10

Since, then, you have been raised with Christ, set your hearts on things above, where Christ is, seated at the right hand of God. Set your minds on things above, not on earthly things. For you died, and your life is now hidden with Christ in God. When Christ, who is your life, appears, then you also will appear with him in glory.
—Colossians 3:1-4

Dear Heavenly Father,
You did not leave me with your commandments and then say, "Go now and do your best to please me." Instead, you gave me your Son, Jesus. You put him on the cross and then after his resurrection, you sent him to live in my heart through the gospel. Now, he lives in me and leads me to do the right things for the right reasons. Help me to lean on these heavenly realities today and not my own morbid strength. What I get from heaven now and what I will have in heaven when this short life is over, is enough to fill my day with peace and joy.
Amen

If you are in Christ, you have endless resources from heaven at your beckoned call. Stop living as if you are a destitute beggar. Everyone in Christ is rich!

Additional Readings: Romans 6, 2 Corinthians 4:16-5:10, Philippians 3, 2 Peter 1:3-11, Revelation 1:4-8

APRIL 11

"What are we accomplishing?" the Pharisees asked. "Here is this man performing many signs. If we let him go on like this, everyone will believe in him, and then the Romans will come and take away both our temple and our nation."

Then one of them, named Caiaphas, who was high priest that year, spoke up, "You know nothing at all! You do not realize that it is better for you that one man die for the people than that the whole nation perish. He did not say this on his own, but as high priest that year he prophesied that Jesus would die for the Jewish nation, and not only for that nation but also for the scattered children of God, to bring them together and make them one. So from that day on they plotted to take his life." —John 11:47-53

Dear heavenly Father,
How painful it must have been for you to watch the unbelieving leadership of your own people plot to kill your Son! The irony of Caiaphas speaking the gospel without even realizing it, must have been a dagger that pierced your soul. Most of the time I do not think of the great pain and sacrifice it was for you as the perfect Father to watch puny human beings intoxicated with their own fabricated importance play devilishly with Jesus. Seeing this now, I know that you feel everything we parents, and grandparents feel when we see our children and their children suffer. You know. You feel. You understand a parent's heart. Be my friend today and guide my parental heart to trust your plans to bring good out of every difficulty my children or grandchildren face just as you knew that the greatest good would come out of the greatest evil done to your own Son.
Amen

You will never be more concerned for the outcome of your children's lives than God is.

Additional Readings: Psalm 23, John 10:27-30, 1 John 3:1-3

APRIL 12

"Then Jesus looked up and said, "Father, I thank you that you have heard me. I knew that you always hear me, but I said this for the benefit of the people standing here, that they may believe that you sent me." —John 11:41-42

Dear Jesus,

I see here that you understand one of my biggest challenges; I doubt that you and the Father are listening when I cry out to you in prayer from my suffering. Sometimes, the silence from heaven is deafening to my faith. But when I read in the above verse that you stood outside of the grave of your friends, Lazarus, and said, "I knew that you always hear me." that's when I knew that you know how hard it is for us sinners who live in front of the curtain blocking us from heaven. You know how we feel so lost when we suffer and pray, and the relief comes so slowly. I will cling to your words here because they assure me that you understand my doubts that your Father is listening to me. Even so, you still want me as your brother in heaven even though I am weak and troubled. Your love and understanding are my strength.
Amen

It is more powerful to be understood and loved by God than to be relieved by him.

Additional Readings: Psalm 50, Psalm 121, Isaiah 65:17-25, Luke 11:1-13

APRIL 13

"I the LORD search the heart and mind to reward each person according to their conduct, according to what their deeds deserve."
—Jeremiah 17:10

Dear Jesus,
This passage confronts me because I know what you will find when you search my heart. I want to live well and for the right reasons. But right there with me is a force, even a very strong force, that pushes me to be selfish and self-pleasing. It is sin living in me! I'm glad you tell me that you're searching my mind, because it makes me deal with the sin in me. But I need your help. First, I need your forgiveness. Then, I need the power to turn my back on the temper tantrums that sin pitches whenever I deny my natural inclinations. Be my Savior today from the guilt and power of this ugly force that challenges me. I trust you will be there for me and so by grace I will have a good day.
Amen

The Lord knows my heart and still rescues me. That's amazing grace!

Additional Readings: Psalm 19, Psalm 1, Hebrews 4:12

APRIL 14

"For my thoughts are not your thoughts, neither are your ways my ways declares the Lord. "As the heavens are higher than the earth, so are my ways higher than your ways and my thoughts than your thoughts. —Isaiah 55:8-9

Dear Heavenly Father,
I have dealt with disappointment so often because my plans for my life didn't become a reality. In those moments, I don't first think that you are doing something good for me that is far above my own reasoning. But you are. This passage helps me let go and let you be God. It leads me to trust that the way my puzzle piece fits into your masterpiece is far better than the way I try to press your plans into mine. Thank you for graciously forgiving me for being angry with you for not cooperating with me and my dreams. Your gracious rule is much better than my selfish ambition. Amen

Don't speak or squirm too soon when you get disappointed. What looks bad now will eventually become very good in God's masterful hand.

Additional Readings: Romans 8:28-39, Isaiah 55:8-13, Ephesians 1:11-12

APRIL 15

For it is by grace you have been saved, through faith — and this is not from yourselves, it is the gift of God — Ephesians 2:8

Dear Jesus,
I often thank you for grace, but I do not as often thank you for the gift of faith in your grace. Faith is not natural for me or anyone else. It's a gift from you. When it comes, I receive peace and confidence to live my life without constant worry and stress. Oh, how often I have fallen from faith and you have used my circumstances and your Holy Spirit to fill me back up. It's a kindness that I cherish from your heart to mine. By your grace I will live by faith today. I'm asking for a new measure of faith today so that I filter every situation I face through the faith grid in my heart and learn to find joy even under the crosses I bear, just as you did when your life was thrust headlong to the cross.
Amen

Keep running as strongly as you can in your weakness while you beg for God to send you life changing faith.

Additional Readings: Psalm 130, Romans 10:10-17

APRIL 16

"If in Christ we have hope in this life only, we are all of people most to be pitied." —1 Corinthians 15:19.

Dear Lord Jesus,
I pray for you to change so many things in the here and now. I seek happiness that comes from relief from suffering and success over struggles. I long to see you act in full view of my five senses. But if you rescue me only for temporary safety, my prayers and your responses are pitifully small. Instead, you give me hope that redefines my whole life and all my prayers. You come to give me life that never perishes. I have hope in you that will never disappoint me. My life is richer today when it is lived as part of the eternity that is already mine. With a heavenly view of my present life, everything takes on different meaning and purpose. Cure me oh Christ, from the eternity amnesia to which I often fall victim. I trust you will answer my daily prayers. But I also trust that if your answer is "no" to any earthly plea, that you still have my seat reserved on the bus to heaven.
Amen

Jesus came to fix my biggest problem and then to work every other problem for my good. Not until I believe this one dual sided truth can I even begin to understand the meaning of his life or mine.

Additional Reading: Romans 8:18-25, 2 Corinthians 4:16-5:10

APRIL 17

Surely God is good to Israel, to those who are pure in heart. But as for me, my feet had almost slipped; I had nearly lost my foothold. For I envied the arrogant when I saw the prosperity of the wicked.
—Psalm 73:1-2

Dear God,
I was born wanting my own way and measuring every experience as good or bad based on that desire. But you came and freed me from playing God and have adopted me into the kingdom of your love and grace. Now I have the choice to be content that I am redeemed, forgiven, and guided by you. Now, every circumstance is a good one, because you promise to work good through them. I have your power to free me from envy of the wicked who succeed so well, even if it is just for a time. Today, I will live in the freedom of not keeping score about anything. I will just live for love and faith.
Amen

Envying a successful pagan is like a schoolboy envying his friend who has a bigger stick of cotton candy. Both big and small cotton candy dissolved in a matter of seconds and give no lasting nutrition.

Additional Reading: Proverbs 24:1-7, Galatians 5:13-21

APRIL 18

One thing I do: Forgetting what is behind and straining toward what is ahead, I press on toward the goal to win the prize for which God has called me heavenward in Christ Jesus. –Philippians 3:13-14

Dear Jesus,
I easily live in the past. I get stuck in regret over my sins, bad decisions, and glaring mistakes or I get caught inwardly gloating over perceived success. But if I do either for very long, I cease to live in the moment with you and this precious moment gets lost in the past. Give me the heart of the Apostle Paul, forgetting that which is behind and seizing today to live in anticipation of heaven. It's your grace that covers my past sins and frees me from my regrets. It's your grace that outshines my past achievements, too. I want to finish strong in your redeeming grace. So, help me preserve the present moment by turning my face toward my final destiny with you.
Amen

Jesus frees us from our entire past so we can live this present moment to the fullest in him.

Additional Readings: Luke 21:25-28, Revelation 1

Donald W. Patterson

APRIL 19

I can do all things through Christ who gives me strength.
Philippians 4:13

Dear Jesus,
I wake up each morning wondering if I will be put in a situation that I cannot handle, and it brings fear to my heart. That's when I preach to myself the sermon of doubt and worry. But when I turn to you and look to your promise that you will never leave me, I realize there is no situation where I am alone. With you in my life, I can face any challenge even if I don't have the answers. I can let you be my wisdom and my strength. So, guide my heart, dear Jesus, into today's great adventure.
Amen

Jesus told us that would always be with us so that would never again think that we had to go it alone.

Additional Readings: Romans 8:37

APRIL 20

So he got up and went to his father. "But while he was still a long way off, his father saw him and was filled with compassion for him; he ran to his son, threw his arms around him and kissed him. "The son said to him, 'Father, I have sinned against heaven and against you. I am no longer worthy to be called your son.'" –Luke 15:19-21

Dear Jesus,
I rejoice that you, the only one who lived in heaven before you were born on earth, would give us this story. You tell us how our Father in heaven feels about us when we are buried in shame and embarrassment over our sins. It's so easy to think that your Father is done with us and our sins. But this story tells me that he's not. The prodigal son had hope that his father would graciously make him a servant. That hope made him go back home. Your Father's love makes me go back home too. The parable gives me hope that when I come home to confess my sin, your Father will run to greet me with grace. This is the most stable influence in my spiritual life. You are the God who cannot hold back your forgiveness when a sinner comes home. I'm home with God the Father because of you Jesus. My goal today is to stay home in your family.
Amen

God wants every single person to come to realize that God really does love them like he loves Jesus.

Additional Readings: Psalm 130, 1 John 3:1-3, Romans 5:15-21

APRIL 21

This is how we know that we belong to the truth and how we set our hearts at rest in his presence: If our hearts condemn us, we know that God is greater than our hearts, and he knows everything.
—1 John 3:19-20

Dear Lord Jesus,
I know that no matter how hard I try or how much I concentrate on improving myself, I will always be severely aware of deep seeded faults that condemn me before your throne. That's why these beautiful words give me a holy, heavenly peace. You are greater than my sin sick heart. Your greatness is found in your ability to forgive it all. I choose to believe what you say about my life instead of what my heart says about it. I am clean, forgiven, restored. Make this peaceful strength drive my heart today.
Amen

Nothing empowers us to face the day better than knowing our gracious God is still behind us.

Additional Readings: Lamentations 3, Romans 3, Psalm 103

APRIL 22

For from his fullness we have all received, grace upon grace. —John 1:16

Dear Jesus,
My whole life has been full of your grace. You spared me from so many disasters that were brewing in my own pot. You gave me opportunities of which I never could have dreamed. You have forgiven me of my entire past. You have promised to forgive me again when I come back with my tail between my legs. You dropped friends by my house when I needed it the most. You have given me an excellent education and understanding of your word. I could list more. All these things are blessings from the fullness of your grace. I can say with John, "God has given me lots of grace." Help me to bless others with the same spirit with which you have blessed me.
Amen

If you truly counted all of God's blessings you would never have time to do anything else.

Additional Readings: Romans 11:36-39, Genesis 32:9-12, 1 Chronicles 29:10-19

APRIL 23

Therefore encourage one another and build one another up, just as you are doing. —1 Thessalonians 5:11

Dear Jesus,
We all need encouragement. I know how much it changes my day when someone gives me a good word. Today, I'm thinking about all those family members who are caring for their aging parents, spouses, or siblings. It's a lonely path with many deep moments of grief. While they make the best of the day ahead of them, help them to bask in the memories of the better days gone by and to reminisce with one another. Also, help them take a journey to the days ahead when we'll all be out of the great tribulation and walk in heavenly glory. Help them to talk about heaven with each other too. Help each caregiver to remember that you see their selfless efforts and how they set aside their lives for those that need them now. Bring the caregivers nearest and dearest friends and other family members to their sides so they will not feel alone or depressed. Help the one they are serving with miraculous relief from their physical problems.
Amen

Loving and serving our family on their last lap is one of God's core values of life.

Additional Readings: Mark 7:6-13, 1 Timothy 5:7-8, John 19:25-27

APRIL 24

Father, if you are willing, remove this cup from me. Nevertheless, not my will, but yours, be done. —Luke 22:42

Dear Jesus,
You had the perfect heart for your Father in the last hours of your life when you prayed. "Not my will but thine be done." I'm glad you prayed so perfectly because you were being my Savior, by living the life I would never manage to live. By your indwelling Holy Spirit lead me to have that same self-sacrificing spirit that yields to our Father's will in every arena of my life. I want to live for the audience of one that you lived for. I want to please him and not just myself. Give me that selfless attitude. Without your converting Spirit I will never even remember what selflessness looks like, much less practice it. So, send your Holy Spirit to change me from the inside out.
Amen

To want what God wants, is a clear mark of conversion.

Additional Readings: 1 Peter 4:1-5, 2 Corinthians 5:11-21

APRIL 25

Call upon me in the day of trouble; I will deliver you, and you shall glorify me. — Psalm 50:15

Dear God,
I need your help every hour of the day. Many problems and challenges overwhelm me. I am listening to your promise in this verse. I am calling to you. Please help me with the issues that loom large in my mind. I cannot do this alone. I am just a small, fallible, finite human being. I believe you will deliver me in your way. I'm not trying to give you any advice. I'm just saying "Mayday!" You take care of the rest. Thanks, not just for being God, but for making yourself my God purely by grace.
Amen

Perilous is the person who has no God to ask for help.

Additional Readings: Jonah 2, Philippians 4:4-7, Matthew 7:7-12, John 15:16, 1 John 5:13-15

APRIL 26

For I desire steadfast love (mercy) and not sacrifice, the knowledge of God rather than burnt offerings. —Hosea 6:6

Dear Jesus,
You quoted this Old Testament passage at least twice in your ministry that we know about. It's a personal core value for you. You want us to show mercy as much as we joyfully receive it. It's so easy to bask in your mercy but throw the law at others. Please, free me from my tendency to punish others with silence, or criticism while enjoying your forgiveness. Help me recall all those that I have been criticizing in my heart and help me to see them close by my side in the shadow of your cross. Make me forget their wrongs by remembering your love. Make the miracle of restoration happen in our relationships. Give me the power to treat them as if they have been the greatest blessing to me.
Amen

We were born deficient of mercy. Only Christ can transfuse it into our souls.

Additional Readings: Matthew 18:21-35, Matthew 9:12-14, Matthew 12:1-14

APRIL 27

"Do not be afraid, little flock, for your Father has been pleased to give you the kingdom." Luke 12:32

Dear Jesus,
I'm often tempted to worry that the world is passing me by as everyone else seems to build better and bigger kingdoms for themselves than I have managed to build for myself. Ah, but all of them are a house of cards, ready to be blown away when you decide it's time to show us who's God. You and the Father have freely given a kingdom to me where blessings, grace, and mercy dwell. It will last when all our man-made kingdoms are destroyed. I love this kingdom. It never passes me by. It always gives me a lift in the royal parade of the redeemed. You have made me royalty. Help me to live as a royal, confident member of your palace today.
Amen

When we know we are royalty and the way back to the palace we don't need anyone else to recognize us.

APRIL 28

Blessed are those whose strength is in you, whose hearts are set on pilgrimage. As they pass through the Valley of Baka, they make it a place of springs; the autumn rains also cover it with pools. They go from strength to strength, till each appears before God in Zion.
—Psalm 84:5-7

Dear Jesus,
The guy who wrote these words for the ancient sons of Korah, was telling us that people lived happy and secure lives (blessed) when they took pilgrimages to your ancient temple to find strength in your word and grace. I have found that same blessed experience whenever I choose meditating on your word and grace as the top priority of my life. As my devotional life goes, so goes my life. But, when I go looking for strength in other things or people, I quickly grow empty, disappointed, and grouchy. Everyone around me pays the price when I'm not finding my strength and value in you. Please, give me the optimism to believe that your word is so great that if I will but spend a little time in it every day, that it will be the medicine that cleans out the spiritual cholesterol coursing through my soul.
Amen

The word of God is the only heart healthy diet for the inner being.

Additional Reading: Psalm 1, Psalm 19, Psalm 119, Psalm 139

APRIL 29

When my heart was grieved and my spirit embittered, I was senseless and ignorant; I was a brute beast before you. —Psalm 73:22

Dear Heavenly Father,
You watch over my whole life. You create good situations for me. Some are learning moments. Others are blessings between a father and his child. All are from your gracious hand. In my mind, I easily become negative in the face of adversity. I look at my empty nets and cry inside. But you are working every situation for my good, even when I cannot imagine what good will come out of it. If I doubt this, I'm like a mere animal and have lost what makes me human, that is; faith. Oh God, don't let me miss the joy of waiting as well as receiving.
Amen

God is more interested in being our heart's desire rather than giving us our heart's desire.

Additional Readings: Hebrews 2:4, Jonah 4:8-11, Lamentations 3:39, Romans 9:20

APRIL 30

"How many times shall I forgive my brother . . . seven times?" Listen to Jesus' reply: "I tell you, not seven times, but seventy-seven times."
Matthew 18:21,22

Dear Jesus,
In my short life I've observed many problems in my family and the families I serve. Those problems have consumed countless hours of counseling and concern. But the biggest problem of all, that too often is left undetected, is the problem of un-forgiveness. We let resentment build between us and our children when they leave their clothes and toys strewn about and don't pick up after themselves when they eat. We get consistently irritable toward our aging parents who are reverting to childish ways because they seem demanding and un-thankful or unaware of the burden, they put on us Our minds replay day after day the selfish things our adult siblings have said or done. We count how many times our spouses have neglected our needs and wants. And we choose cold indifference over vital loving relationships. You have given us the solution. From the cross you forgave everyone of everything, and this opens the door for you to have a relationship with all people. Give me the power of your gospel to fully and freely forgive my family and to pursue deep forgiving relationships with them.
Amen

Forgiveness is the most wonderful vacation anyone could ever take. It's a vacation from the monotony of resentment.

Additional Readings: Ephesians 4:32, Colossians 3:12-17, Luke 23, Revelation 7:9-17

MAY 1

Now listen, you who say, "Today or tomorrow we will go to this or that city, spend a year there, carry on business and make money." Why, you do not even know what will happen tomorrow. What is your life? You are a mist that appears for a little while and then vanishes. Instead, you ought to say, "If it is the Lord's will, we will live and do this or that." —James 4:13-15

Dear Lord,
How often I live as a practical atheist, making plans without a thought about you running my life but all the while expecting you to bless what I want you to bless. My life is yours. Everyone's life is yours. The whole universe is yours. So, here, take back the steering wheel and guide my life in every detail. I believe you when you say that you will turn everything for my good, even when I never accomplish my goals. With the freedom that comes from faith, I choose to live this day for your glory and the good of others.
Amen

Disappointment dissipates when our expectations are for God forgive our messy mistakes instead of to bless our messy plans.

Additional Readings: Proverbs 3:5-6, Ecclesiastes 3, Psalm 90

MAY 2

Now listen, you who say, "Today or tomorrow we will go to this or that city, spend a year there, carry on business and make money." Why, you do not even know what will happen tomorrow. What is your life? You are a mist that appears for a little while and then vanishes. Instead, you ought to say, "If it is the Lord's will, we will live and do this or that." –James 4:13-15

Dear Lord,
How often I live as a practical atheist, making plans without a thought about you running my life but all the while expecting you to bless what I want you to bless. My life is yours. Everyone's life is yours. The whole universe is yours. So, here, take back the steering wheel and guide my life in every detail. I believe you when you say that you will turn everything for my good, even when I never accomplish my goals. With the freedom that comes from faith, I choose to live this day for your glory and the good of others.
Amen

Disappointment dissipates when we expect God to guide and forgive our hearts instead of to bless all our plans.

Additional Readings: Proverbs 3:5-6, Ecclesiastes 3

MAY 3

"If we are faithless, he remains faithful, for he cannot disown himself."
— 2 Timothy 2:13

Dear heavenly Father,
It has taken me a long time to realize and believe in my everyday practical heart that your commitment to accepting, guiding, sustaining, and blessing me is totally dependent on who you are as the faithful God. It's not one iota dependent on who I am or how well I am performing as a Christian. I would have no lasting relationship with you at all if you were not 100% committed to loving me. But since you are faithful, I feel happy and contented today. My guilt is gone, my fear is quieted, and I trust how you will work this day out for my good. What a great mystery that you would be a friend of sinners.
Amen

When I am close to God, I worry about human friendships a whole lot less.

Additional Readings: 1 John 3:19-21, Lamentations 3:23, John 16:33

MAY 4

May the God who gives endurance and encouragement give you the same attitude of mind toward each other that Christ Jesus had, so that with one mind and one voice you may glorify the God and Father of our Lord Jesus Christ. —Romans 15:5-6

Dear Lord,
Sometimes I am frightened by the challenges I face. I think there is no way I will endure through it all. It seems too big for me. I forget that you are the God who gives endurance and that you never intended for me to carry my burden alone. You have always wanted to be the God to whom I look for help. So, Lord, I know you see the mountain that I see in front of me. From your heavenly perspective, it looks like a foothill. Reach down today and make me a strong enduring person of God who steps bravely onto the side of the mountain to traverse its heights. Now, my fear is giving way to hope as I remember that you are right here with me. Amen

When you walk with God you get to ride on his shoulders whenever you need a little break.

Additional Readings: Psalm 90, Psalm 91

MAY 5

"As Christians we are sorrowful yet always rejoicing; poor, yet making many rich; having nothing, and yet possessing everything."
–2 Corinthians 6:10

Dear Lord,
Thank you for transporting my soul into your kingdom. Here, I live enriched by your grace, promised help, and final glorious destiny. All the while, my body lives in the challenges and tragedies of this life. So, I can have real joy even while I grieve over my earthly losses. I can have real wealth while being challenged by my limitations, and real hope even when I know my days are short. I love to tell the story of how you have created the alter-world of salvation and peace for all who would dare to trust in you.
Amen

As God's people we never have to live one day in hopelessness.

Additional Readings: 2 Corinthians 1, 4 and 5

MAY 6

After Jesus was born in Bethlehem in Judea, during the time of King Herod, Magi from the east came to Jerusalem and asked, "Where is the one who has been born king of the Jews? We saw his star when it rose and have come to worship him." –Matthew 2:1-2

Dear Jesus,
On this day, we remember the Magi who came from a faraway culture to worship you when they knew so very little about your person and work. Help me to remember that the resolution to all my problems is not in some secret knowledge or spiritual skill that I learn to master. Instead, it is found in you, my God and Savior, who loves me more than anyone else does and who has mastered my life better than the same.
Amen

Additional Readings: 1 Corinthians 1:18-31, Colossians 2

To be a Christian is to willingly stop worshiping yourself and to actively worship Jesus Christ for who he is and what he does.

MAY 7

Someone in the crowd said to him, "Teacher, tell my brother to divide the inheritance with me." Jesus replied, "Man, who appointed me a judge or an arbiter between you?" Then he said to them, "Watch out! Be on your guard against all kinds of greed; life does not consist in an abundance of possessions." –Luke 12:13-15

Dear Lord,
I always thought greed was found in those who indiscriminately accumulate. But it's also found in me when I complain about what I did not get. I am embarrassed over the many hours I've spent thinking about personal economics and whether I should be concerned, upset, or pleased with this or that financial situation in my family, work, or country. Your words, "Life does not consist an abundance of possessions" are heart searching. Oh, how the "good life" could rob me of "real life." Soon, I must walk away from all of it. You have created me for eternity. Forgive me for trying to live for this short earthly life. I beg you to free me from all the pains and thrills I let overtake me regarding the heap that is soon to be distributed to others.
Amen

Whoever has the most toys when they die will probably lose.

Additional Readings: Matthew 6, 2 Corinthians 8,9

MAY 8

And the wise men came into the house, they saw the young child with Mary, his mother. And they fell down and worshiped him. They presented to him gifts of gold, frankincense, and myrrh. —Matthew 2:11

Dear Jesus,
These wise men knew that you were the God who had come to earth to solve all our problems. They didn't know how you would die and rise again. But they trusted you as a person. I don't know how you will solve all my problems either. But I trust you as a person and I give you my gifts and worship just like they did. Thank you for the wisdom to recognize you for who you are and to let go of the details. If there is anything you want me to do to help myself or someone else and I am missing it, please show me what to do. reveal the path to me the way you did to those wise men.
Amen

We trust a person not just a doctrine or a revealed plan.

Additional Readings: Psalm 25, Genesis 50, Ephesians 1:11

MAY 9

And there were shepherds living out in the fields nearby, keeping watch over their flocks at night. An angel of the Lord appeared to them, and the glory of the Lord shone around them, and they were terrified.
—Luke 2:8-9

Dear Heavenly Father,
It's a terrifying thought that we would face you in all your glory and give an accounting for our lives. We feel this deeply when we think that death is immanent. We are never ready for the sifting of a lifetime of thoughts, words, and actions. That's why the words, "Do not be afraid ... a Savior is born to you" are so comforting. Your angels appeared in your glory to tell us that you sent your Son to be accountable for our trashy lives. Oh, how that makes me love you! I'm ready to face you because your Son faced me and said, "I've got this!" Thanks for the Christmas spirit of substitutionary grace.
Amen

Jesus faced the most unfair life anyone would ever live, so we could face his Father with a clean slate.

Additional Reading: Hebrews 2:5-18, 1 Corinthians 15

MAY 10

For the grace of God has appeared that offers salvation to all people. It teaches us to say "No" to ungodliness and worldly passions, and to live self-controlled, upright and godly lives in this present age, while we wait for the blessed hope—the appearing of the glory of our great God and Savior, Jesus Christ, who gave himself for us to redeem us from all wickedness and to purify for himself a people that are his very own, eager to do what is good." – Titus 2:11-14

Dear Jesus,

I wish I could say that sin looked horribly ugly and destructive to me, but it doesn't. I wish I could say that I hate sin the way you hate it, but I don't. I wish I could say that I always love to do what is right, but I don't. I wish I could say that I always think your way is better than my way, but I can't. I wish my heart was always happy to stay within your Father's boundaries, but it isn't. It's hard to admit it, but sin often looks attractive, relieving, and satisfying to me. That's why I need your Holy Spirit and your restorative grace. If you did not pursue me, change me, and push me in the right direction, I would self-destruct. I am as vulnerable today as the first day I came to faith. Oh, Jesus, stay near me forever and love me I pray.
Amen

To need God is human.

Additional Reading: Hebrews 10

MAY 11

"A time is coming and in fact has come when you will be scattered, each to your own home. You will leave me all alone. Yet I am not alone, for my Father is with me. "I have told you these things, so that in me you may have peace. In this world you will have trouble. But take heart! I have overcome the world." –John 16:32-33

Dear Jesus,
You are honest with us. You and the Father chose to fix the people and not the world in which we live. As I face my sadness and struggles this day, please walk by my side and make your presence known. Give me the peace of knowing that you love me, you have a good plan that finds its fulfillment even through the web of "bad" things you weave into our lives. Help me to learn whatever it is you are teaching me and to be the light and love for those who are troubled next to me. Give me so much love that I am free from asking myself, "What about me?" or "Why is this happening to me?" and instead to ask, "What can I do for this or that person to make their lives better?"
Amen

It's easier to do something to alleviate some pain in the lives of those around us when we know Jesus will soon alleviate all their pain.

Additional Readings: 2 Corinthians 1:3-11

MAY 12

I pray that the eyes of your heart may be enlightened in order that you may know the hope to which he has called you, the riches of his glorious inheritance in his holy people, and his incomparably great power for us who believe. That power is the same as the mighty strength he exerted when he raised Christ from the dead and seated him at his right hand in the heavenly realms – Ephesians 1:18-20

Dear God,
Ever since you forced your way into my life, I have been happier, more grounded, more content, more honest, more prone to grow, more compassionate, wiser, more self-disciplined, more compliant, more peaceful, more gentle, more hopeful, more faithful, more loyal, and more of what you have always wanted me to be. Your powerful grace has carried me forward from that very moment. Thank you for choosing me from eternity to meet your Son in this era of all time and to give my life meaning and purpose that the passing world could never produce. I am impressed that you tell me that the power you have used to change my life is the same power you used to raise Jesus from the dead. It connects me to Christ more intimately and it makes the meaning of Christmas and Easter that much deeper.
Amen

Once God saves a soul he then sets out to change it.

Additional Reading: Romans 6, Ephesians 3:14-21

MAY 13

"For he himself is our peace. Who has made the two groups one, and has destroyed the barrier, the dividing wall of hostility, by setting aside in his flesh the law with its commands and regulations. His purpose was to create one humanity out of the two thus making peace.
—Ephesians 2:14-15.

Dear Jesus,
When you removed our impending judgment by your sacrifice you also removed the persistent judgment that divides us from one another. It's not that we should not judge each other according to the law because according to the law we could all condemn one another and not be wrong. But since you have satisfied God's law you have also given us the privilege to let go of the sins of others that offend us. Help me to live in the shadow of your cross today and from there to forgive everyone that would otherwise drive me crazy with disappointment and anger. Use your love to remove the dividing wall between me and all other people.
Amen

Grace from God creates indestructible relationships between people.

Additional Reading: Proverbs 16:7, Isaiah 56:1-7, Romans 4

MAY 14

"I lift up my eyes to the mountains — where does my help come from? My help comes from the Lord, the Maker of heaven and earth.
— Psalm 121:1-2

Dear Lord,
Sometimes I am overwhelmed with how vulnerable my family and I are to sickness and trouble. Trying to anticipate every challenge and to fix every dilemma will at times raise my blood pressure. That's why your reminder through David in this psalm is so heartwarming. I can look away from myself to you and get your supernatural help. You are God. I am just a small integer in your infinite universe. You know what is worrying me today. I'm asking, even begging you, be my God and deliver me and my loved ones. Help us and guide us in what to think and do.
Amen

The human heart was made to depend of the heavenly Head.

Additional Reading: John 15, Acts 4:23-31. 1 John 5:14

MAY 14

You desired faithfulness even in the womb; you taught me wisdom in that secret place. – Psalm 51:6

Dear Lord,
At the very beginning of my existence in my mother's womb, you desired faithfulness from me. You want an honest life where I acknowledge you as Creator and lover of my soul. You desire me to sincerely search for truth and practice love. In the secret most inner chamber of my soul I know that I have been wayward and selfish way too much. I am sorry. I beg for your forgiveness and ask you to make me whole again in your mercy. Cover my life with the life of your Son and make me an honest and repentant follower. With my remaining days create in me a clean heart that desires what you have always desired and that finds great joy in living solely for you and not myself.
Amen

Everyone knows deep down that God wants them to be as truthful as he is.

Additional Readings: Proverbs 9:10-12, Proverbs 12:22-24, Ephesians 4:25

MAY 15

"Therefore, since the promise of entering his rest still stands, let us be careful that none of you be found to have fallen short of it. For we also have had the good news proclaimed to us, just as they did; but the message they heard was of no value to them, because they did not share the faith of those who obeyed." —Hebrews 4:1-2

Dear Jesus,
You came to give me rest anytime, anywhere, no matter how much stuff I must do or what intense meetings await me. Your rest is a rest within because you settle me on the truth that I am loved. I am forgiven. I am blessed. I am safe and I am important. All this you proved to me by giving your very life for me. I believe you are right here with me today. Give me that rest in my soul and stop me from looking for it in a change of my situation or my relationships with people. And from that rest make me an instrument of peace of rest for others.
Amen

When we rest in God on the inside we can rest in life on the outside.

Additional Readings: John 14:27, 16:33, Hebrews 12

MAY 16

"Lord, the Lord Almighty, may those who hope in you not be disgraced because of me; God of Israel, may those who seek you not be put to shame because of me. – Psalm 69:6

Dear Heavenly Father,
You know all my weaknesses and foibles and you covered my shame when you put your Son on the cross. By your grace and your Holy Spirit, give me the strength to resist all temptation and to do those things that bring honor to my family and the body of believers. I do not want to bring shame on you or your people or my people. Help me be a reason for them to hold their head up and not down. Give me a confident attitude of obedience and faith so I am a strength and not a drain on others.
Amen

In the shadow of the cross is light to make one shine for the God of grace.

Additional Reading: 1 Thessalonians 1, Titus 2:11-14

MAY 17

Since the children have flesh and blood, he too shared in their humanity so that by his death he might break the power of him who holds the power of death—that is, the devil—and free those who all their lives were held in slavery by their fear of death. For surely it is not angels he helps, but Abraham's descendants. For this reason, he had to be made like them, fully human in every way, in order that he might become a merciful and faithful high priest in service to God, and that he might make atonement for the sins of the people. Because he himself suffered when he was tempted, he is able to help those who are being tempted. —Hebrews 2:14-18

Dear Jesus,

It will always blow my mind that you willingly left heaven to take on flesh and blood and live 33 tough years on earth in order to free us wayward sinners from our greatest enemy, death. And here in Hebrews, you remind me that while you were here, you experienced temptation and the stress and challenge it causes just like we do. You want me to know that you empathize with my weaknesses; I can come to you for help again and again without being judged. You never raise an eyebrow at me. Be with me today and help me overcome my temptations. Be with me and help me deal with my doubts and fears. Be with me today and help me find happiness amid sorrow and disappointment. Make my day different by your gracious presence, no matter what it holds for me. Amen

When you know He loves you with an everlasting love, you aren't afraid to be yourself in his presence.

Additional Reading: John 10, 1 John 3:1-3

MAY 18

The Lord is gracious and compassionate, slow to anger and rich in love. The Lord is good to all; he has compassion on all he has made.
—Psalm 145:9-10

Dear Heavenly Father,
I love to hear that you are compassionate and slow to anger. I know that I could anger you every day. But you deal with me with a tender heart and hands. I also love to hear that you have compassion on all that you have made. Even each sparrow garners your attention. This thought overwhelms me with awe and appreciation. Today will be a good day because I live it under you watchful and loving eye. Do not let me fall into sin or run into any kind of danger and in all I do help me to do what is right in your sight. Make me more compassionate to all people and creatures, as well.
Amen

No Christian is fatherless. No believer is an orphan.

Additional Reading: Psalm 37, Psalm 103, Psalm 104

MAY 19

"If we walk in the light, as he is in the light, we have fellowship with one another, and the blood of Jesus, his Son, purifies us from all sin."
−1 John 1:7

Dear Jesus,
I know that you see all our thoughts and so, on your part, you are in perfect harmony with each of us. The light of your omnipresence shines into every soul. But between me, a sinner, and all the sinners around me, the light of understanding is rather dim. I long for deeper and more honest and grace-based relationships. But without our strong belief that your grace covers our sins, doubt and fear will keep us from being open with each other. Please help me and those near me to translate the relationship we have with you into deep and meaningful relationships with each other. Purify us from our sinful and wayward hearts. Tear down the fortress of anxiety and fear. Give us the strength to venture over the mote of silence to share life changing communication with each other.
Amen

God sees every deep-rooted thought in your soul. People only see the flower, whether it is withered or in full bloom.

Additional Reading: Jeremiah 17:5-10, Ephesians 4:17-32

MAY 20

"Cast all your anxieties on God because he cares for you." 1 Peter 5:7

Dear Jesus,
I bet your disciples loved to let go when you were around. They knew you could handle anything from a wine-less wedding to a squalling storm at sea. But I can't see you, so I forget that you are there and care enough to help me with all my troubles and problems. Right now, I give you all my worries and fears. Handle the pressure for me. Tell me what you want me to do and I will do my part. But you shoulder the results.
Amen

When God picks up his end of the log, my end becomes featherweight.

Additional Reading: Joshua 1:1-9, Psalm 139

MAY 21

The fear of the LORD is the beginning of wisdom and knowledge of the Holy One is understanding. – Proverbs 9:10

Dear Lord,

It's a lifelong battle in my soul to honor, love, and fear you more than I honor myself. But often you flex your muscle and the world around me trembles. That's when I realize afresh that I am in your world and not you in mine. Everything in my life makes more sense when it's dwarfed by your presence. I understand better how to live and how to make good decisions. My goal is to know you, understand you, respect you, and love you. But I often forget. Forgive me, for Jesus' sake, and do not stop coming back to get me. If it were not for your constant love reaching out to me, I would be ruined. Please walk beside me today. I need your presence, guidance, and grace.
Amen

Remember how your dad struck both fear and confidence in your young heart? That's what it's like to walk with God.

Additional Reading: Psalm 104, Psalm 130, Romans 8:14-39

MAY 22

But you, Lord, are a shield around me, my glory, the One who lifts my head high. I call out to the Lord, and he answers me from his holy mountain.
I lie down and sleep; I wake again, because the Lord sustains me.

I will not fear though tens of thousands assail me on every side
— Psalm 3:3-6

Dear Lord,
As I hear more and more about the activity of evil men and other random crazy people in my "village" I find myself more fearful for myself and my family. Then I think of all the diseases and accidents that can assail us and I get nervous. The spiritual answer is to do what your psalmist does here. I will tell you about my fears and I will lay my need for protection at the foot of your throne. Oh, Lord, be my shield and cover my life with your angels at least three deep around me. Protect me and keep my loved ones safe, too. Since I have given you the charge of being my great protector, I will not spend any more energy worrying about it. Instead, I will throw myself into loving and serving my family and friends. Show me someone that I can shelter today. And make me thankful and not envious as I live with all the blessings you give me.
Amen

Worry and envy are fraternal devilish twins that rob the soul of life and vitality. Slay them each day with faith in your benevolent God.

Additional Reading: Hebrews 13

MAY 23

Sanctify them by the truth; your word is truth. —John 17:17

Dear Jesus,
You said these words the night before you died in your prayer to your Father. They have been a light for my path ever since I discovered them. The way that you teach my heart is by your word. Everyone has their own opinion and frankly many of them sound very good although they are very wrong. Your word gives me heaven's opinion of all things. They have rung true in every circumstance even when what they say hurts me. They always bless me in the end. Help me to digest your word deeply today and to apply it to the challenges I'm facing so that I act out on earth what you desire from heaven. Guide me in your truth.
Amen

There is no worthy substitute for the truth regarding any matter on earth, from rocket science to personal relationships.

Additional Reading: Psalm 25, Psalm 119

MAY 24

Behold, the hour is coming and indeed has come when you will be scattered, each to his own home, yet I am not alone. For, the Father is with me. —John 16:32

Dear Jesus,
The lonely road I walk through life, no one who fully understands. Being left alone with all my thoughts, feelings, and emotions is sometimes too much to bear. I know it was not originally meant to be this way, but it is for every one of us. You experienced loneliness more than all of us when you were here. You felt aloneness but you told us that you were not alone. The presence of your Father comforted you. You understand my aloneness. Don't let it turn to loneliness. You and my Heavenly Father and the Holy Spirit see my every thought and understand me even better than I do myself. I find comfort in knowing you are with me close by on the journey and that you can touch my frustration of being alone. So, I pray, fill me with your presence and drive out loneliness from my life so that I reach past myself to bless others with friendship.
Amen

The fall into sin makes everyone lonely at times. Jesus makes everyone loved all the time.

Additional Reading: Psalm 139

MAY 25

This is the day the LORD has made. Let us rejoice and be glad in it!
—Psalm 118:24

Dear Heavenly Father,
Some of us are at the beginning of life with so many unanswered questions. Others are in the middle where we are so busy, we forget things and miss important moments. Still others have only one question to answer; "Will this be my last day or will it come tomorrow?" But this one common denominator we all have together. We all have today as a gift of your grace. We all have your promise of an eternal tomorrow. We all have a past riddled with blessings to sort through when we are bored. We all have hope and peace and love in your Son. This is a day of good times and we will learn to be thankful in it.
Amen

Living in the moment as a thankful child of God is an act of faith.

Additional Reading: Psalm 37

MAY 26

The Lord was with Joseph so that he prospered, and he lived in the house of his Egyptian master. —Genesis 39:2

Dear Heavenly Father,
Had you not been with Old Testament Joseph all his problems would have ended poorly. But you never left his side and therefore every problem was used to work some good. You promise to never leave my side either. So, I know that you will prosper me in ways I could never imagine. Life will be good and fulfilling if I have you with me. That's all that matters. In the optimism that comes from knowing you are with me; I start my day with you. Bless my heart with insight along the way, my hands with productive things to do, and my mouth to speak hope to others. Bless those you send to help me, also. Make them useful and happy in their service to others. In all our lives, show the world that you are the God who saves.
Amen

We don't need to know what will happen next. We just need to know God will be in the 'next' with us.

Additional Reading: Philippians 2:1-11

MAY 27

If the law had been given that could impart life, then righteousness would certainly have come by the law. But Scripture has locked up everything under the control of sin, so that what was promised, being given through faith in Jesus Christ, might be given to those who believe. – Galatians 3:21-22

Dear Jesus,
I trust that you have saved me completely. As hard as I may try to live a good life, it will never get me safely to the other side. You have done that for me. When I think about living right at the present time, I want to work at it in order to say thanks to you. I do not think I am earning your love or attention. But here is my problem, I still try to earn my own self-respect and when I sin it takes me too long to get over my own self condemnation. Help me Jesus to follow your lead and forgive myself the second I discover my failings so I can live in love without the distractions of self-criticism and guilt.
Amen

Care not what you think but what God thinks, and your life will make sense.

Additional Reading: Hebrews 4:12, Jeremiah 17:5-17

MAY 28

The highest heavens belong to the Lord but the earth he has given to humanity. — Psalm 115:16

Dear Lord,
We all run around this globe and compete for our little piece of the pie. But truly, the whole earth is a gift to all of us from you. We get to use it for our short lives and then we must let go of it to others. What a wonderful gift from you. Every flower, every tree, every mountain, every sunrise and sunset, all of wildlife and domestic creatures, even the people you allow me to live with; they all point to you. You are an amazing creator and benevolent donor of all things. Today, I will enjoy my little corner of your world with its multifaceted blessings and I will worship you in my heart because you are the author of it all.
Amen

Creation is never an end. It always is the means which God uses to bless us and to draw us to himself.

Additional Reading: Psalm 19, Psalm 53, Romans 1:18-22

MAY 29

But now in Christ Jesus you who once were far away have been brought near by the blood of Christ. For he himself is our peace, who has made the two groups (Gentile and Jew) one and has destroyed the barrier, the dividing wall of hostility. . . . His purpose was to create in himself one new humanity . . . and in one body reconcile them both to himself through the cross, by which he put to death their hostility.
—Ephesians 2:14–16

Dear Jesus,
You removed all hostility that exists between your Father and people and any hostility that exists between sinners who hurt one another. In that single, solitary act of dying for both perpetrator and victim, you reconciled everyone in all directions in one instant. Help me take what you did for us on the cross and make it the reason and the power that I declare myself reconciled to the people who have hurt me or let me down. Use your gospel to remove the hostility between people I don't like and me for my own "good" reasons. Give me peace that makes me boldly live in the presence of folks that give me the willies. Give me the cross shaped love that keeps me from being unhappy to see anyone. Use your salvation to save me from my own unhealthy aloneness.
Amen

In heaven you will have the joy of not being angry with anyone. Why not get a head start and stop being angry now?

Additional Reading: Genesis 50, Matthew 6

MAY 30

Many times God delivered Israel, but they were bent on rebellion and they wasted away in their sin. Yet he took note of their distress when he heard their cry; for their sake he remembered his covenant and out of his great love he relented. He caused all who held them captive to show them mercy. Save us, Lord our God! – Psalm 106:43-47

Dear Heavenly Father,
Too often I have viewed your discipline as punishment for my sins. I'd have thought that you were expressing harsh rejection and dissatisfaction. But I know now that your harsh punishment for me was exhausted at the cross of your Son. So, when I hit a hard time, sometimes because of my sin and sometimes as a training ground under your love, I see it as acceptance and love not rejection and irritation. I would not have this insight without your word. Thank you for showing me today that you had the very same relationship with Israel. Because of your eternal covenant of love for her, you kept rescuing and disciplining. Help me find security in the discipline I experience from your hand, because in Christ, everything is good.
Amen

Love is not unbroken approval of our actions but unbroken acceptance of our whole being.

Additional Reading: Hebrews 12

MAY 31

There was a man sent from God whose name was John. He came as a witness to testify concerning that light, so that through him all might believe. He himself was not the light; he came only as a witness to the light.

The true light that gives light to everyone was coming into the world. He was in the world, and though the world was made through him, the world did not recognize him. –John 1:6-10

Dear Jesus,
I know that you will keep sending special people into my life too bless me and help me grow just like you sent John the Baptist. When they come, help me not to expect too much from them. It's easy to think that they should give me more than they are capable. There is only one you, one Savior, one author of my soul. In gratitude for the family, friends, and leaders you give me, I will live in peace with their failings and I will look to you for things that only a god could give. That way I will not resent their humanness. Be my light today so I reflect your love and truth to myself and others.
Amen

People cannot let you down if you do not raise them up.

Additional Reading: 1 Corinthians 3, Psalm 1

JUNE 1

For now we see only a reflection as in a mirror; then we shall see face to face. Now I know in part; then I shall know fully, even as I am fully known. —1 Corinthians 13:12

Dear Jesus,
Even your apostle Paul, who was inspired to teach us things unseen, lived his life without knowing many answers to his deepest questions. You tell us all that we need to know, but not all that we want to know. We cannot handle the answers to every question. Help me to accept this and then to let go of all the unanswered questions in my life. It's enough just to know that you are the Author, the Provider, the Savior, and the welcoming party at the end. I want to rest in faith and not perfect knowledge. I give to you all the stress of trying to make sense out of tragedy. When I get to where you are, you can tell me more. And when I get there, I still won't need to know everything. Just to know you more than today will be enough.
Amen

Wanting to know why instead of wanting to know love is a major character flaw in us all.

Additional Reading: Galatians 5, 1 John 4

JUNE 2

Oh Lord, teach us to number our days that we might gain a heart of wisdom ... Establish the work of our hands, yes, establish the work of our hands. Psalm 90

Dear Heavenly Father,
You have already planned the length of my life. Sometimes, I live as if I will be here forever and I know deep down that's not true. Help me to do the right things and the important things today, so that this day, which otherwise seems insignificant, will take its proper place in a meaningful life. Use your supernatural power to make even the insignificant moments to have an impact down the road in a positive way. And I pray for all my friends and family that are between jobs. Remind them that you have their next job waiting for them and that you will make today meaningful even though they are not employed by some human entity.
Amen

For a believer every day is a gift exchange with God.

Additional Reading: Ecclesiastes 1-3

JUNE 3

My God will meet all your needs according to the riches of his glory in Christ Jesus. —Philippians 4:20

Dear Father in Heaven,
What Paul told the Philippians is true for me, my family, and my friends. You will meet all of our needs. You won't hold back because of our sins and you won't miss any of our needs by being distracted. So, I have chosen to give up worrying about anything today. I give all my needs and wants to you. I know you care for me and I know you will come through at exactly the right time. Help my friends and family to let go of worry also. Give them peace that their mental mulling squirrel cage could never give. Help us all find the peace that comes from trust.
Amen

God never feels unprepared to meet our needs.

Additional Reading: Matthew 6:19-34

JUNE 4

Our citizenship is in heaven. And we eagerly await a Savior from there, the Lord Jesus Christ, who, by the power that enables him to bring everything under his control, will transform our lowly bodies so that they will be like his glorious body. —Philippians 3:20–21

Dear Lord Jesus,
In recent months I have had to sit by and watch as the bodies of my nearest and dearest friends failed them until finally their soul was released to you. It's the most difficult experience in our lives. It reminds me that my turn to let go of my borrowed space is nearer. If it were not for your short life, death, and resurrection, I would be hopeless and unable to enjoy anything. The thought of the end would rob me of joy. Your gracious gift of rescue is my dearest friend and it becomes more precious to me as each loved one passes. Help me to live in the hope of heaven today and to reflect this hope to all those who are suffering from the deep disappointment that comes from the loss of a dear one.
Amen

Be happy. Because of Jesus we will have the time of our lives once the time of our lives is over.

Additional Reading: Luke 21:25-28, Hebrews 2:5-18

JUNE 5

Therefore as we have opportunity, let us do good to all people especially those that belong to the family of believers. – Galatians 6:10

Dear Jesus,
Today, help me see my deep connection to the entire human family and to own the happiness and needs of fellow humans as my own personal mission. Help me to leave behind selfish ambitions and singular, personal goals that are only all about me. In my heart set aside your bride, the church, as my own sacred family so that I deeply serve every believer I know from a mind enlightened by your grace and truth, not counting our differences as worthy of a passing glance.
Amen

No one is too small or too far gone for Jesus to love them through us.

Additional Reading: Ecclesiastes 11, Mathew 25:31-46, James 2:1-13

JUNE 6

And the Lord's servant must not be quarrelsome but must be kind to everyone, able to teach, not resentful. Opponents must be gently instructed, in the hope that God will grant them repentance leading them to a knowledge of the truth, and that they will come to their senses and escape from the trap of the devil, who has taken them captive to do his will. —2 Timothy 2:24-26

Dear Jesus,
I want to stand up for the truth and help sinners find their way back to you, but I do not want to be a rude know it all that always picks a fight with everyone. Help me to set my heart on winning people over with gentle prodding instead of clubbing them with my frustration. When I am with my family, help me to encourage them so they feel their heart overflowing. When I need to defend your truth help me to protect their feelings while I correct them, so they are attracted by the beauty of love as much as he brightness of truth.
Amen

Love is powerful, gentle, and life changing, but never brash or rude.

Additional Reading: Galatians 5:22-23, 6:1-5, Philippians 4:4-9

JUNE 7

My flesh and my heart may fail, but God is the strength of my heart and my portion forever. — Psalm 73:26

Dear Heavenly Father,
Although I do many things to love and care for the body you have given me, it's going to fail me. Up until now, it has only partially failed me, but I know the hour is coming when no matter how badly I want to stay here, my body will check out on my soul. But you will never check out on my soul. You have redeemed me, and you promise to raise me up with a restored and renewed body on the last day. You are my portion and my strength forever, oh God. You will hold me close to you even when my body will make it hard for others to look at me. This makes me love you more than life itself.
Amen

Our souls never age, never die, have no gender or race and are dearly loved by the one who created them.

Additional Reading: Luke 23:39-43, 2 Corinthians 4:16-5:10

JUNE 8

Give us today our daily bread. –Luke 11:3

Dear Lord Jesus,
I confess that I spend too much time living in the past and evaluating all my decisions and disappointments. When I dwell on the past, I'm not looking up to you and what you promise me today. The past has no bearing on the fact that you are going to give me what I need for today. Help me to let go of the past when I pray the Lord's Prayer, "Give me today my daily bread." Thank you that you have covered the past, even yesterday, with your life, death, and resurrection. Your life cuts my life free from my failures. The release enables me to enjoy a good day under the sunshine of your grace. I know you will bless my body and soul with all that I need for today.
Amen

When you look up to Jesus, you can see past every dark cloud.

Additional Reading: Hebrews 13:5-5, Matthew 6:19-34, Psalm 37

JUNE 9

Finally, be strong in the Lord and in his mighty power. – Ephesians 6:10

Dear Jesus,
I always seem to get myself into trouble when I feel strong and confident. I believe it's because, too often, I'm feeling strong in myself without you. Then, by myself, I do something rambunctious and I hurt others or myself. I want to be strong in you. I want your gentle, firm strength to speak the truth forcefully but in love, to be a support for others but not in my own strength, to be a beacon for the weak and troubled but not to be their Savior. Will you give me that strength today so that when I am weak, I am strong?
Amen

True spiritual strength is a gift from Christ and not a force or a philosophy.

Additional Reading: Colossians 2

JUNE 10

"I, even I, am the Lord, and apart from me there is no savior. I have revealed and saved and proclaimed— I, and not some foreign god among you. You are my witnesses," declares the Lord, "that I am God."
—Isaiah 43:11-12

Dear Heavenly Father,
There is so much pressure today in the news, in high schools, universities, and in the general public to believe that all faiths are the creation of human minds springing from our culture and our need for security. These voices want to mute the offensive and beautiful message that you are the only true God and that you want all humanity back under your redeeming grace. Help me not to believe the muting lie that all faiths are equal. You are the only God for me and everyone else. Give me boldness to challenge everyone who is lost around me with your confrontational love.
Amen

When you know you are loved by someone perfectly, you will show it by your boldness in defending their reputation, God included.

Additional Reading: Isaiah 8:16-22, Romans 1:18-32

Donald W. Patterson

JUNE 11

Heaven and earth will pass away but my words will never pass away.
Matthew 24:35

Dear Jesus,
Thank you for reminding me of the terribly temporary nature of this world and everything which make sentimental. Make me sentimentally attached to your word and the insights they teach me. Today, help me recall the verses you want me to have for the challenges and opportunities that lay before me. Do not leave me alone with my temporal things.
Amen

Sooner or later everything except God and people end up being sold at garage sale values.

Additional Reading: Psalm 1, Psalm 119

JUNE 12

"You will not certainly die," the serpent said to the woman. "For God knows that when you eat from it your eyes will be opened, and you will be like God, knowing good and evil." When the woman saw that the fruit of the tree was good for food and pleasing to the eye, and desirable for gaining wisdom, she took some and ate it. She also gave some to her husband, who was with her, and he ate it. 7 Then the eyes of both of them were opened, and they realized they were naked; so, they sewed fig leaves together and made coverings for themselves.

Dear Heavenly Father,
The devil is a beast in conversations with my soul. He calls you a liar and puts thoughts of distrust in my heart. At the same time, he tempts me to be independent and to decide for myself what is good for me and what is right or wrong. When I fall for his tales, I find myself naked with guilt and shame. Oh, please lead me not into temptation by him. I am no match for him. Hold your cross in front of my eyes to clothe me in its shadows. I have never found anything else that will free me from the guilt and shame of having acted selfishly. Thank you for this deep hearted salvation.
Amen

Only with God in our corner can we stay in the ring with Satan.

Additional Reading: James 1:2-18, James 4:7-10

JUNE 13

This is the account of the heavens and the earth when they were created, when the Lord God made the earth and the heavens. ... The Lord God said, "It is not good for the man to be alone. I will make a helper suitable for him." So the Lord God caused the man to fall into a deep sleep; and while he was sleeping, he took one of the man's ribs and then closed up the place with flesh. Then the Lord God made a woman from the rib he had taken out of the man, and he brought her to the man.
—Genesis 2

Dear God,
Marriage is your creation, your institution, your beautiful gift to humanity. And humanity has made a mess and a mockery of it ever since the fall. In my generation, it is treated as the creation of humans who can abide by it or ignore it on a whim. I am confessing the sins of our entire generation. We have lost our way regarding this beautiful creation of yours. Help me to live in reverent thankfulness regarding my own marriage and to give that solitary person nearest to me the satisfaction of a happy marriage. Give me the insight to meet the needs of my wife so that she enjoys marriage as you wanted her to.
Amen

Great human beings are not those who neglect marriage to conquer some worldly goal. They are the humble servants who strive to make God and family happy in God pleasing ways.

Additional Reading: 1 Peter 3:1-7, Ephesians 5:21-33

JUNE 14

But do not forget this one thing, dear friends: With the Lord a day is like a thousand years, and a thousand years are like a day. The Lord is not slow in keeping his promise, as some understand slowness. Instead he is patient with you, not wanting anyone to perish, but everyone to come to repentance. – 2 Peter 3:8-9

Dear Heavenly Father,
Today I am not only thankful that you are so patient with me but also that you are patient with all those I love and hold dear who have wandered away from you. I know that you are patient with the whole world and that makes me trust your love even more. Make me patient like you so I am there for everyone no matter how far they have fallen.
Amen

Patience is the first leaf sprouting out of mercy.

Additional Reading: Matthew 5:2-12

JUNE 15

He will also keep you firm to the end, so that you will be blameless on the day of our Lord Jesus Christ. God is faithful, who has called you into fellowship with his Son, Jesus Christ our Lord. –1 Corinthians 1:8–9

Dear Father,
Thank you for promising that you have given me your Son to fellowship with in the word and prayer. I have his support and help to make it through this life and to the end with my faith intact. I am convinced that if you did not give me the help I need from Jesus and the Holy Spirit, who work through your word and the church, I would be a wandering sheep who traveled from one hill to another far away from you and the truth. It gives me peace knowing that your plans and schemes to keep me close to you are endless.
Amen

Sheep who are prone to wander underestimate the creative and radical methods God will use to ultimately bring them home.

Additional Reading: Luke 15

JUNE 16

"At one time we too were foolish, disobedient, deceived and enslaved by all kinds of passions and pleasures. We lived in malice and envy, being hated and hating one another. But when the kindness and love of God our Savior appeared, he saved us, not because of righteous things we had done, but because of his mercy. He saved us through the washing of rebirth and renewal by the Holy Spirit, whom he poured out on us generously through Jesus Christ our Savior, so that, having been justified by his grace, we might become heirs having the hope of eternal life." – Titus 3:3-7

Dear Lord,
Although I have grown up in the faith since being a small child, I can still remember times when I forsook your grace and presence and lived as Paul described Titus' friends, a victim to passion and plagued by bitterness. But your kindness and love has rescued me from that dog eat dog mentality. As an heir of yours, I have all I need to feel settled, rich, and benevolent. I want to share this "wealth" of soul with whomever I meet. Help me to view everyone today as a soul who needs the overflow of love that you have poured into me. Make me gentle, kind, and encouraging. And when I do not know how to encourage them, help my loved ones who are suffering to find their wealth in you while they battle the challenges you have let them face too.
Amen

Christ's love has made us rich in generosity so that we freely give without fear of losing anything.

Additional Reading: Romans 12

Donald W. Patterson

JUNE 17

I am confident of this, that he who began a good work in you will carry it on to completion until the day of Christ Jesus. —Philippians 1:6

Dear Lord Jesus,
It's a tough pill to swallow that this is not paradise and that I am not the knight in shining armor ruling over it. But the spoon full of sugar that helps this medicinal truth go down, is that you are fashioning me into the person you want me to be. Because you are ever present in all the resources you have put in my life like family, friends, coworkers, education, challenges, and most of all your Holy Spirit who brings grace and truth to me every day. Therefore, I have contentment and hope. I am content with my less than perfect circumstance and I am hopeful that life is looking up and finally will end in glory where I will find the paradise for which I long. Today will be a good day because of the contentment and hope you have given me during my fallen life. AMEN

God and God alone, can rescue me from the dimwitted depression that results from dreams not ever fully realized.

Additional Reading: Philippians 3

JUNE 18

If we claim to be without sin, we deceive ourselves and the truth is not in us. If we confess our sins, he is faithful and just and will forgive us our sins and purify us from all unrighteousness. If we claim we have not sinned, we make him out to be a liar and his word is not in us.
—1 John 1:8-9

Dear Jesus,
You have made a way for me to drop all defense mechanisms when you send people to point out my weaknesses and mistakes. Give me the courage to admit my faults to myself and others and to cash them in for full and free forgiveness from you. Then help me live in the power of grace without obsessing with regret about the repeated nature of my sins. Help me to live a happy spiritually forgetful life because I live under the new covenant created by you. AMEN

Daily grace breaks us free from daily guilt like daily showers wash away daily dirt.

Additional Reading: Jeremiah 31:31-34

JUNE 19

Set your minds on things above, not on earthly things. For you died, and your life is now hidden with Christ in God. When Christ, who is your life, appears, then you also will appear with him in glory.
—Colossians 3:2–4

Dear Jesus,
Here is the secret to me overcoming any foible, temptation or sin; I am to think about how you have rescued me from sins' power and guilt and to reckon myself dead to the temptation or the guilt. I claim that you have erased it all through your perfect life and death. This seems too good to be true, but I find it works when I trust you enough to try it. Frankly, Jesus, telling myself about your forgiving love is much more wonderful self-talk then the brow beating guilt that one can so easily cycle through. I like thinking about you and your rescue much more than I like thinking about my sins. Thank you for being my Savior.
AMEN

The next decision you make is much more important than any you have already made.

Additional Reading: Galatians 3

JUNE 20

The seed falling among the thorns refers to someone who hears the word, but the worries of this life and the deceitfulness of wealth choke the word, making it unfruitful. —Matthew 13:22

Dear Jesus,
You hit the nail on the head with this one. I love your word and I believe that life is all about you, and at the same time I let worries about this life and the deceitfulness of American affluence choke out my peace and purpose as a light for you. It's a terrible roller coaster for me, often making me spiritually nauseous. What really bugs me is that my own personal dreams become a need in my heart, and I get an artificial unhappiness if I can't reach them. Please free me from this and give me the richness of a heart set on you and the joy of serving others. Make me like you when you triumphed over life and death by the way you lived free from the thorns of worldly success.
AMEN

If you get stuck on an earthly dream, you will doom yourself to disappointment.

Additional Reading: Luke 12

JUNE 21

Do not repay anyone evil for evil. Be careful to do what is right in the eyes of everyone. If it is possible, as far as it depends on you, live at peace with everyone. —Romans 12:17-18

Wow, God,
These two little verses give me clear, hard hitting direction for my conduct in relationships. You don't want me to give anyone the silent treatment and you don't want me to use sarcasm to get even. You want me to live in such a way as not to bring shame on your name in front of anyone. You want me to seek peace in relationships and not my own way. There are two big things that must happen. First, I must kill my natural man. Because naturally, I want to get even and live recklessly. Secondly, I must be filled with your Spirit, because without you, I am doomed to follow my natural inclinations. Oh, Lord Jesus, come and save me from myself today and to spare others from having to endure my dark side others.
AMEN

The pursuit of peace and love is enough to make every day a meaningful challenge.

Additional Reading: Ephesians 4

JUNE 22

I, wisdom, dwell together with prudence; I possess knowledge and discretion. I love those who love me, and those who seek me find me
— Proverbs 8:12,17

Dear Heavenly Father,
I am tempted to pursue many things to make me happy. But in the end, it's always your truth and wisdom that satisfy my soul. Help me to remember that getting insight from you is more valuable than any other accomplishment. Help me to want to understand my life from your perspective more than from my own. Help me to seek peace with you more than peace with myself. Help me to see in your Son all that I need right here and right now to give my life meaning, purpose, and value. Give me the daily "hand out" of spiritual wisdom today so that every unfinished conversation and uncompleted task does not haunt me because I know that I have your completed life covering mine.
AMEN

Objective truth and wisdom exist apart from us. Seek them out and do not rest until you find them in God.

Additional Reading: Psalm 25

JUNE 23

"Be still and know that I am God." Psalm 46:10

Dear Father in Heaven,
You are the center of the universe, not me. That's both liberating and confrontational at the same time. Forgive me for the deeply rooted belief that I struggle against which says I must be everything I need. I am NOT God of myself or anyone else. So, I give you the steering wheel. Take my life where you wish. I will lightheartedly just look out the window at all the beautiful sights.
Amen

Want a never-ending vacation? Then let God be God of your life.

Additional Reading: Mark 6:3-56

JUNE 24

Some trust in chariots, some in horses, but we will trust in the name of the LORD our God! – Psalm 20:7

Dear Heavenly Father,
I am tempted to triple check the lock on my doors before going to bed at night. My generation and culture put great faith in guns as home protection. I often think that airbags and seat belts are my assurance of salvation. But no matter what devices I use, I cannot put my hope in any of them. My hope for protection is on you. You promise to keep me safe, to work difficulties to my advantage and to finally take me to glory. Help me to walk by this faith and not by sight. Give me the sense today that you are with me wherever I go so that I am free from worry and fear. Help me to focus on serving others without much concern for myself.
AMEN

Serve others dangerously. God has your back!

Additional Reading: Jeremiah 17:5-10

JUNE 25

I plead with Euodia and I plead with Syntyche to be of the same mind in the Lord. Yes, and I ask you, my true companion, help these women since they have contended at my side in the cause of the gospel, along with Clement and the rest of my co-workers, whose names are in the book of life. —Philippians 4:2-3

Dear Lord Jesus,
I have often read these verses how Paul begged the church to help these women get along with smug self-righteousness, thinking, "How immature they must have been." But, deep down I know that his plea applies to me, too. I get the old saying, "To dwell above with saints I love will be glory. But to dwell below with saints I know, that's another story." Help me see every family and church member as people whose names are written in your book. Help me to cross the bridge over the moat between us to reconcile with those with whom I have differences. Give me a heart that wants to fill my short life with warm, messy relationships instead of cold, neat, and tidy isolation and cohabitation. Make your good news the glue that holds us together.
AMEN

The truth in every relationship is in the middle.

Additional Reading: John 13

JUNE 26

Bear with each other and forgive one another if any of you has a grievance against someone. Forgive as the Lord forgave you. And over all these virtues put on love, which binds them all together in perfect unity.
—Colossians 3:13–14

Dear Lord,
I sometimes think that if I have a legitimate reason to be angry with someone, then I also have a legitimate reason to withhold forgiveness. In this passage, you tell me that I am responsible to forgive even if I have a legitimate complaint. That means, the minute they sin against me, I have a new job to do unrelated to them. It's between you and me. I am supposed to forgive in the same way that you forgave me. This is hard to remember and even harder to implement once I remember it. But, if I will keep my eyes on you a not the person who hurt me, then I can let go because my life is a "Christ" thing and not a "me" or "them" thing. Oh, Jesus, help me be a Christian. I cannot do this without you.
AMEN

Forgiveness is pouring out what you have taken in, not producing what you never had.

Additional Reading: Ephesians 4

JUNE 27

You will keep in perfect peace those whose minds are steadfast, because they trust in you. —Isaiah 26:3

Dear Lord,
It's not change that I hate. It's change that forces me to live in new painful realities that I despise. Like when very dear friends start down that steep hill of physical decline and I must watch them grieve over needing more help than they give. The 180-degree switch is gut wrenching. But I have learned from them what you mean in this passage. I have learned from them to find peace in your promise to forgive, to relieve, to restore and to raise back up at the last day. I have seen the peace of the gospel wash over them and I know that it's because they trust in you. Hold your cross before our tired eyes so we never forget that the last great change for us will be the best one.
AMEN

No matter how far the downturn is today, the last turn is always up for the child of God.

Additional Reading: Isaiah 41:1-20

JUNE 28

For who knows a person's thoughts except their own spirit within them? In the same way no one knows the thoughts of God except the Spirit of God. —1 Corinthians 2:11

Dear Heavenly Father,
There is a secret room in my heart that no one understands but me. I find great comfort in knowing that you have the same room in your heart. None of us fully understand you. I am honored that you chose to tell us many of your secrets through the Holy Spirit, whom you sent to create the written word. When I take time to study your words carefully, I see things about you that make me understand and appreciate you for who you are and for how much you love us. Thank you for sharing Christ with us from that secret room. And thank you for creating us with the ability to have a secret room for ourselves. Give us wisdom on how we manage who gets to see inside that holy place.
AMEN

It's in the secret room in each person's heart that one knows whether he is truly worshiping God from faith and love.

Additional Reading: 1 Corinthians 2

JUNE 29

To the pure, all things are pure, but to those who are corrupted and do not believe, nothing is pure. — Titus 1:15

Dear Lord,
I am intrigued and challenged by this verse. Your purifying grace changes me and the way that I look at everything and everyone else. Instead of critical and condemning thoughts, your grace gives me pure love and an ability to see the value in every sinner, because they are a soul you died for. You help me see that any rules I make have no power to change me, others, or our situation together. Only grace and truth can change any of us. Help me see that when I get down on others and am overcome with angry thoughts about them, that I have fallen from grace. And on the flip side, help me to live a changed life filled with honesty and love toward everyone; a love that comes faith and not rules.
AMEN

The gospel does through us what our complaining and arguing constantly fails to produce.

Additional Reading: James 3 and 4

JUNE 30

Are not five sparrows sold for two pennies? Yet not one of them is forgotten by God. Indeed, the very hairs of your head are all numbered. Don't be afraid; you are worth more than many sparrows.
—Luke 12:6-7

Dear Jesus,
I love this illustration you use to calm my soul. I see so many sparrows every day. They are such small and vulnerable creatures, but you care for each one. If you have so much care for such an insignificant little creature, I know that I have your full concern. It helps me let go of worry about anything. When changes happen in my life that threaten to make my life harder and more complicated, it's easy for me to get anxious, down, and depressed. Your words pull me up out of that pit. My life has meaning, direction, stability, and hope because it's owned and governed by you, my loving Savior. Wow, what a big difference a few words from your lips can make!
AMEN

Pastor Don Patterson

Worry in a Christian is a remnant of congenital atheism.

Additional Reading: Matthew 6

JULY 1

A person's steps are directed by the Lord. How then can anyone understand their own way? – Proverbs 20:24

Dear Lord,
We spend most of our lives in the dark about what is going to happen to us and those we love. You have forced us to take it as it comes. Even our own decisions are overseen and ordered by your providential will. This "predicament" used to cause me great anxiety, but as you have revealed more and more of your love and wisdom to me, I have come to enjoy being blissfully ignorant of the outcomes toward which you lead us. Since I have come to know you as my God, my Father, and my friend, I am learning to trust you in the craziest of circumstances. Please help my friends and family that stay "freaked out" by what's happening around them, find peace in trusting your love to oversee their journey.
AMEN

If Jesus came to pick you up for a long road trip, would you worry about how the trip was going to turn out?

Additional Reading: Psalm 23

JULY 2

Don't you know that you yourselves are God's temple and that God's Spirit dwells in your midst? If anyone destroys God's temple, God will destroy that person; for God's temple is sacred, and you together are that temple. —1 Corinthians 3:116-17

Dear Lord Jesus,

I can see from your words through Paul that you are very serious about the unity of your church because it is the living temple where you dwell. It makes me shudder to think how many times I have used critical words about another Christian or Christian leaders. I repent of saying things that destroy your temple, the church. Give me the wisdom and courage to speak to the people I am concerned about and to do it with love and humility. Because I love you and am so thankful that you brought me to faith through your church, I want to build it up wherever I go. Help me to talk to people and not about them. Give me the wisdom to help others make this their mission, too.
AMEN

Pastor Don Patterson

When we love God, we love his church, also.

Additional Reading: 1 John 4 and 5

JULY 3

Rejoice in the Lord always. I will say it again: Rejoice! Let your gentleness be evident to all. The Lord is near. Do not be anxious about anything, but in every situation, by prayer and petition, with thanksgiving, present your requests to God. And the peace of God, which transcends all understanding, will guard your hearts and your minds in Christ Jesus. —Philippians 4:4-7

Dear Jesus,
I want the joy that comes from serving you which cannot be affected by outer circumstances. I want the gentleness that comes from not needing to have every person changed and every problem resolved. I want that peace that transcends all understanding. You promise it comes when I turn everything over to you in prayer. I give you all my concerns that I have about loved ones. I give you all my concerns about my own problems. Take my life an d let be yours to guide and protect.
AMEN

When you give your problems to God don't go back and try to reclaim them.

Additional Reading: Psalm 31

JULY 4

Why do you look at the speck of sawdust in your brother's eye and pay no attention to the plank in your own eye? How can you say to your brother, 'Let me take the speck out of your eye,' when all the time there is a plank in your own eye? You hypocrite, first take the plank out of your own eye, and then you will see clearly to remove the speck from your brother's eye. –Matthew 7:3-5

Dear Jesus,
I must be honest with you. You see my soul even better than I do. I am bugged more by other people's sins and weaknesses than my own. And I am often more desperate to see them change than I am to welcome changes for me. I like telling them how they can change too, and I don't like it when they tell me how I can change. That's why your words are so powerful for me. They turn the table around. So, what are the planks in my heart? By your Holy Spirit, give me the ability to see them when others are trying to tell me what I need to change. More importantly, give me the power to admit them to myself and to accept the uncomfortable feelings that come with change. Then, as I understand, three dimensionally, how hard change is, I trust you will help me to be more tender and precise in how I dare to point out the speck in someone else's life. Hold my hand and help me through this dear Savior.
AMEN

Do us all a favor and don't avoid the mirror in the morning or the mirror in your closest friends.

Additional Reading: Ephesians 4

JULY 5

Let us not become weary in doing good, for at the proper time we will reap a harvest if we do not give up. Therefore, as we have opportunity, let us do good to all people, especially to those who belong to the family of believers. —Galatians 6:9-10

Jesus,
Sometimes I get weary and tired of serving people, especially when it seems I have no effect on their well-being. It's at those times I am tempted to fantasize about quitting to seek a life of seclusion and self-interest. I need your help. Rescue me from the quitter inside. And rescue all my friends and family from the quitter in them, too. Give them the joy and strength to take care of their aging parents and love them when they start acting like children. Help moms of little kids who sap their energy and wear them out with endless messes and demands. Help dads not quit on helping those moms and help friends be there for each other, too. We need you every hour to be our strength to love people until our last moment.
AMEN

Pastor Don Patterson

No one can love people perfectly like Jesus did, but everyone can learn to let Jesus love others through them.

Additional Reading: Philippians 2

JULY 6

Wealth is worthless in the day of wrath, but righteousness delivers from death. — Proverbs 11:4

Dear Father,
I live in a land that is addicted to money. Every day, I see headlines about boatloads of money someone earned or lost. Voices are constantly reminding me to prepare for the short time I will not work at the end of my life, ... money, money, money! It's so easy to believe that it defines security. But it cannot do anything for me on that day when I stand before you to give an accounting for my life. Then only righteousness will help me. With all the money I have, I am fresh out of righteousness every day. I need you every hour to cover me with your Son and his perfection. Thank you for giving me the spiritual money I will need to pay the debt I will owe at the end. Now, I can live my life with hope and peace today. Money can be a tool for me and not a god.
AMEN

How much money you shared out of faith will be more important on judgment day than how much you saved for yourself.

Additional Reading: Ecclesiastes 11, Malachi 3

JULY 7

Dear friends, let us love one another, for love comes from God. Everyone who loves has been born of God and knows God. 8 Whoever does not love does not know God, because God is love. ...Everyone who believes that Jesus is the Christ is born of God, and everyone who loves the father loves his child as well. —1 John 4:7-8 and 5:

Dear Heavenly Father,
I have seen how much you love me and it has made me love you without fear. In loving you, I want to put you back on the throne of my life. From there, you tell me to love others. Especially those that are your children. I easily love some of them, but I suspect you wrote this word because I don't love all your children. That's right Father, I want to blame them for how hard they are to love. But the truth is, they are hard to love because I still have a long way to go in my faith and understanding of your grace and truth. Give me the power to love those that I struggle to love. Make someone who wonders if I love them be delightfully surprised by what happens between us today.
AMEN

When having a hard time loving another, look for the answer in God and not your own unloving heart.

Additional Reading: 1 Corinthians 13

JULY 8

Speaking the truth in love, we will grow to become in every respect the mature body of him who is the head, that is, Christ — Ephesians 4:18

Dear Heavenly Father,
When I think of all the conversations that went poorly from my end, I can attribute their demise to one of two mistakes. 1) Either I did not speak truthfully, OR 2) I did not speak lovingly. That's why I love your simple word from Paul. By "speaking the truth in love," it gives all of us the best opportunity to grow up into the likeness of Jesus. He always spoke the truth in love. And his truth, in love words, still change us today whenever they are read. Help me to find my voice and be honest today with everyone I meet and don't let a selfish or harsh tone come out of my mouth. Only let me speak what will build others up in their life of faith and service to you and others.
AMEN

They charge fines for littering on the highways. So, don't litter people's minds with poorly chosen words either.

Additional Reading: James 3

JULY 9

"You will not certainly die," the serpent said to the woman. "For God knows that when you eat from it your eyes will be opened, and you will be like God, knowing good and evil." When the woman saw that the fruit of the tree was good for food and pleasing to the eye, and also desirable for gaining wisdom, she took some and ate it. She also gave some to her husband, who was with her, and he ate it. —Genesis 3:4-6

Dear Lord,
It is hard to think about, but when I look at this account of the first moment when a human sinned, I see myself. When I buy into the lie that you cannot be trusted, that's when I look at everything around me and decide for myself, based on my own incomplete wisdom, that I can do this or that, think this or that, or say this or that. It's like jumping off the platform of faith onto the huge spiral water slide of sin and guilt. The ride is fun for a few moments and then it leaves me feeling empty and gives me so many more thoughts and problems to work through. So, build up my trust in you, O Lord, so that I listen, trust, and obey rather than go off on my own trusting only myself. Today, point out to me one place you see me doing this and lead me out of temptation to the higher ground of faith and obedience. Give me the courage to tell myself "NO!" Thank you for saving my sinful soul through your redeeming grace.

Temptation is the lie that you can sin without ever feeling any consequences.

Additional Reading: James 1

JULY 10

Be still before the Lord and wait patiently for him; do not fret when people succeed in their ways, when they carry out their wicked schemes.
—Psalm 37:7

Dear Lord,
The matters over which I have no control really bother me. When I hear in the news that a godless agenda is being shoved down our throats, I get very anxious. When at work I can tell that someone is selfishly scheming for their own advantage and not honestly trying to do good, my blood boils. It makes me wonder where you are or if you are listening when you tolerate the schemes of sinners. But, this verse redirects my heart. I can be still before you and wait for you to work out your good and righteous plan even through allowing the selfish schemes of others. I will calm down and wait because you tell me that you are in control even when I cannot see the immediate effects of it. I'm glad you are God and I'm not.
AMEN

When good or evil happens around you, don't think too hard or too soon, otherwise you might be living in an imaginary outcome prematurely.

Additional Reading: Psalm 37

JULY 11

Put to death, therefore, whatever belongs to your earthly nature: sexual immorality, impurity, lust, evil desires and greed, which is idolatry. Because of these, the wrath of God is coming. You used to walk in these ways, in the life you once lived. But now you must also rid yourselves of all such things as these: anger, rage, malice, slander, and filthy language from your lips. Do not lie to each other, since you have taken off your old self with its practices and have put on the new self, which is being renewed in knowledge in the image of its Creator. —Colossians 3:5–11

Dear Jesus,

If I carefully read through this list, I still see things I must consciously renounce today even after following you for over three decades in adulthood. I have learned socially acceptable ways to practice some of these vices. But, I know in my heart they are not acceptable to you. Give me the wisdom to see the subliminal ways that my heart leads me into the dark woods of selfish living. I want out of the revolving door of endless bickering and struggles to get what I want or think I need. You can rescue me. Grab me by the hand and take me safely in the right direction. Lead my heart to selfless contentment.
AMEN

Happiness is not a destination that we pursue. It is a gift that surprises us when we meet Jesus.

Additional Reading: Romans 8

JULY 12

For although they knew God, they neither glorified him as God nor gave thanks to him, but their thinking became futile and their foolish hearts were darkened. —Romans 1:21

Dear Lord,
I know you are amazing because life is amazing and complex. You are the Supreme Being that made me and everything I see around me. You own us all. I just want to say, "Thanks." Thanks for the opportunity to share life with some very loving people. Thanks for the brilliant folks you have blessed to make things happen for me and my family, like the airplane that brought me home, the government that insures my safety, and the smart phone that makes me feel stupid. Thanks for the gospel that restores me from my fallen place and for friends that never cease to remind me that your unconditional love is alive and well in them by the way they have forgiven me.
AMEN

Gratitude is the only response worthy of the privilege of opening your eyes again this morning.

Additional Reading: Psalm 150

JULY 13

I tell you that in the same way there will be more rejoicing in heaven over one sinner who repents than over ninety-nine righteous persons who do not need to repent. —Luke 15:7

Dear Lord,
I cannot fully fathom how you and all of your angelic friends value each and every soul on this earth. I am tempted to care for only a few people that also care for me. I see others as obstacles in the way on my journey to happiness. Oh, how far my heart can be from the beatings of your heart's passion. Give me the passion for the redemption of lost souls that you and the angels have. I want to know by experience the deep celebration that happens when we own the eternal welfare of another human being as our inner ambition and get to see their moment of salvation.
AMEN

To love another human being the way God and his angels do, is a miracle of faith.

Additional Reading: Revelation 21 and 22

JULY 14

And when you pray, do not be like the heathen... but when you pray, say "Give us this day our daily bread." –Matthew 6

Dear Jesus,
I see two main points in this prayer that you have given us. 1) You want me to look to you and not myself to provide everything I need for this body and life. 2) You want me to ask for it daily and not plan for a storehouse that will pile up a hundred times more than I will ever need. Both points for truly praying "give me daily bread" lead me to repentance for wanting to be God of my own life and provider of everything I would ever need. It's a hard petition to honestly practice. I hear voices telling me I need to worry about all my future in this passing world as if it all depended on me. Give me the faith that you are telling me to have, so that I will ask you for what I need each day. I want to fully trust that you will be a loving Father and give it freely to me and those I love.
AMEN

Praying for daily bread while worrying about tomorrow is being two faced with God.

Additional Reading: 2 Corinthians 8 and 9

JULY 15

God was in Christ reconciling the world to himself. – 2 Corinthians 5:19

Dear God,
Today will be a good day for me because I know you are not mad at me about anything. You have already reconciled yourself to me. I have the freedom to live transparently before you and others and have the hope of your help and grace. Thanks for being the perfect father.
Amen.

Grace is the X factor in every believer's life.

Additional Reading: 2 Corinthians 5

JULY 16

Oh, the depth of the riches of the wisdom and knowledge of God! How unsearchable his judgments, and his paths beyond tracing out!
—Romans 11:33

Dear Heavenly Father,
When I was just knee high to a grasshopper and my parents took us on our annual summer two-week vacation, I knew very little about the cost, the preparations, the map or the blessings they were intending us to receive from their planned journey. I was free to concern myself with who got the window seat and if my little sister's blanket was touching me or not. I really was just along for the ride. I think back on those times with great peace. I was well parented. I had it made. I fall back on those feelings of contentment when my present journey gets crazy. I have had very little to do with so much about my journey. I am in your car on the journey you have chosen for me. Keep me in the back seat while you drive! Help me to look out the window and take in the countryside because you are watching the road. Give me the peace of a well parented child. And when you surprise me with a challenge help me anticipate the blessing beyond the present struggle, so I do not lose hope.
AMEN

God is driving your life. The sooner you quit jerking the wheel the sooner you both start enjoying it more.

Additional Reading: Psalm 139, Romans 11

Donald W. Patterson

JULY 17

Jesus Christ is the same yesterday, and today, and forever. —Hebrews 13:8

Lord Jesus,
I marvel at how so many of the things you give all people are the same. We all have the same air to breath, the same birth, life, death process. We all have the benefits of water and light and four seasons. (Okay, well some of us have two.) We all have the same moral law written in our hearts and the same bible as an anchor for our souls. And here you remind me that we all have the same you. You are the same for my generation and me as you were for my parents, grandparents and all the others before me. Today, I want to be so aware of how we are all equally gifted by you that I kick my envy and striving for more to the curb while I lose myself in giving people something extra because you made sure they encountered me.
AMEN

You will never be God's greatest gift to anyone, but you will be the icing on the cake for a few.

Additional Reading: Acts 17

JULY 18

In your relationships with one another, have the same mindset as Christ Jesus: Who, being in very nature God, did not consider equality with God something to be used to his own advantage; rather, he made himself nothing by taking the very nature of a servant, being made in human likeness. And being found in appearance as a man, he humbled himself by becoming obedient to death — even death on a cross.
—Philippians 2:5-8

Dear Jesus,
It's liberating to know that since you have come into my life that my attitude and emotions are no longer a captive of my circumstances. With you in my jail cell, I can choose to live like you in humility and love even when I feel slighted, hurt, vengeful or angry. It's very comforting to know that I can acknowledge those feelings and the people and incidents that cause them and then simply fold them up and put them away in a box while I lose myself in loving everyone, even my enemies. It's invigorating to think that nothing and no one can really dictate how I feel except you and your promises. Help me to remember all of this when I step out of my home today because I'm used to forgetting it around 10:00 am every day. Give others the light of your love by helping me to remember to choose a good attitude.
AMEN

When in doubt act like Jesus until you figure it out.

Additional Reading: 1 Corinthians 13

JULY 19

It is for freedom that Christ has set us free. Stand firm, then, and do not let yourselves be burdened again by a yoke of slavery.
—Galatians 5:1

Dear Lord Jesus,
In This month that we celebrate the divine privilege of living under the freedom of western democracy, I am overwhelmed with thanksgiving that I also get to live in the freedom of complete and total forgiveness. Many people died to purchase my American freedom but you alone died to purchase my spiritual and eternal freedom. I am among the most fortunate people who have ever crawled around on the earth. I will honor you each day by living in positivity, contentment, thankfulness and happiness. I have the distinct blessing of being free both in my country and in my soul. I'm free to pursue life my own way in my country and free from guilt, shame and fear in my soul.
AMEN

Christian Americans are the freest people who have ever graced the planet.

Additional Reading: Romans 13

JULY 20

Be devoted to one another in love. Honor one another above yourselves. Never be lacking in zeal, but keep your spiritual fervor, serving the Lord. Be joyful in hope, patient in affliction, faithful in prayer. Share with the Lord's people who are in need. Practice hospitality.
—Romans 12:10–13

Lord,
Strengthen my devotion to family, especially aging relatives who need so much more of my support and the young who take more energy and guidance. Help me to be patient in the afflictions caused by everyday life and the aging of my own body. Help me to daydream not so much about what more affluence would look like for me, but about what more love would like for others. Give me ideas of someone new that I could practice hospitality for. Fill me with a servant's heart that changes the lives of others with your warm presence working through my imperfect life.
AMEN

Faith daydreams more about what love looks like for others than about what wealth looks like for self.

Additional Reading: Galatians 5 and 6

JULY 21

"When you pray, do not be like the pagans, but pray ... 'Thy kingdom come!'" –Matthew 6:6,10

Oh, Heavenly Father,
I am tired of being on the throne. I willingly yield it to you. Just a warning though; there is more to get done and to fix in my little kingdom than one man could ever do. I thought I was man enough to do it all, but alas, I was not. The harder I tried, the messier it got. I'm afraid to throw so much at you since you are already ruling so many other things, but then again, you are God. You can handle it and you tell me that you want to handle it too. Now that I am not all stressed out running the show, what small parts do you want me to concentrate on? I like this. I will help you as you lead my life, instead of allowing you to help me as I lead myself. Thy kingdom come ...
AMEN

There is room for only one king in the throne room of your heart and it's not you.

Additional Reading: Revelation 21 and 22

JULY 22

"Do not seek revenge or bear a grudge against anyone among your people, but love your neighbor as yourself. I am the Lord.
—Leviticus 19:18

Dear Jesus,
The temptation is there to find subtle ways to get even with those close to me while I rehearse all the reasons they deserve it. It's easy to justify withdrawing love from them if they are careless or selfish around me. My sins may not be news worthy but I know you see my conniving ways. Forgive me and by your grace reach down and make me emotionally mature enough to act in love and not revenge in even the slightest ways. I want my family and friends to know that you are alive and well by what they see in me.
AMEN

Selflessness and aspirin have this in common: they both reduce pain.

Additional Reading: Romans 12

JULY 23

Rejoice with those who rejoice; mourn with those who mourn. Live in harmony with one another. —Romans 12:15-16

Dear Lord,
It is so hard for us sinners to get out of our own little worlds to truly and deeply rejoice with those who have happy things going on their lives and to truly and deeply hurt out loud with those who are experiencing struggle and tragedy. But your Holy Spirit who lives in our hearts drives us with this passage to make sure that others are not alone in their joy or their sorrow. Give me the mojo I need to make me "be there" with people whom I know are experiencing one of these two extremes. I don't want to avoid feeling their pain or their joy because of my selfish instincts to protect myself. Use your love to make me really live the fully connected life.
AMEN

Christ's love in our lives makes us too busy with people to be lonely.

Additional Reading: Matthew 20

JULY 24

If we claim to be without sin, we deceive ourselves and the truth is not in us. If we confess our sins, he is faithful and just and will forgive us our sins and purify us from all unrighteousness. If we claim we have not sinned, we make him out to be a liar and his word is not in us.
–1 John 1:8–10

Oh God,
It is counter intuitive for me that if I give up excuses, denial and hiding I will find relief, a clean conscience and peace. My natural mind wants to fix what I have broken without any help because that way I could be proud of my own power to improve. But there is no fixing what I have done. I'm a sinner and I can point to several ways I have sinned recently. I admit them. I'm sorry. I need your forgiveness and cleansing! And ... I believe your promise. In Christ you have removed them all! I am out of hiding and I can live honestly before you and others. Thank you for the light of true spiritual repentance and renewal. Help those clinging to their sin to come out of their closet too, not to celebrate but to repent and be washed by the grace you so freely share.
AMEN

Repentance is created by God through his promise to forgive.

Additional Reading: Jonah 2, Romans 2

JULY 25

It is the glory of God to conceal a matter; to search out a matter is the glory of kings. – Proverbs 25:2

Dear Jesus,
Our culture has lied to us by making us think that we have a right to know what is going on in everyone else's lives. They love to make a story out of the evil things others do. They keep the attention off of you and the powerful grace you are spreading everywhere. And I have suckered for it. As all of my peers, I have developed an appetite for tantalizing news that distracts me from more wholesome thinking and living. Give me the power to diet from all of the "breaking stories". Help me to settle down to serving real relationships with real durable love and commitment. Give me the strength to live my own reality with you in the middle of it all covering my sins and erasing guilt and shame.
Amen

The devil likes to get us to say "wow" at bizarre sin. God likes to get us to say "wow" at redeeming, purifying, changing grace.

Additional Reading: Genesis 50

JULY 26

Do not store up for yourselves treasures on earth, where moths and vermin destroy, and where thieves break in and steal. But store up for yourselves treasures in heaven, where moths and vermin do not destroy, and where thieves do not break in and steal. For where your treasure is, there your heart will be also. —Matthew 6:19–21

Dear Jesus,
This is a hard one. I have never been to heaven and no one I know who is still on earth has either. So, we all get tied to the things of this earth as if they constitute wealth and security. But in fact both savers and spenders are fools if they do not consider that it will all be removed from their lives eventually. You are my greatest treasure and I already have all of you. Help me to live in peace knowing I have everything when I have you. And give me the wisdom and courage to speak to others about you. I want to lay up treasures in heaven and there is no greater treasure to you than people.
AMEN

Hoarding money on earth is like feeling really rich when you win at Monopoly. At the end, both winner and loser walk away and re-enter reality."

Additional Reading: Psalm 24, Psalm 100, Psalm 145

JULY 27

Surely God is good to Israel, to those who are pure in heart. But as for me, my feet had almost slipped; I had nearly lost my foothold. For I envied the arrogant when I saw the prosperity of the wicked. They have no struggles; their bodies are healthy and strong. They are free from common human burdens; they are not plagued by human ills. Therefore, pride is their necklace; they clothe themselves with violence.

This is what the wicked are like — always free of care, they go on amassing wealth. Surely in vain I have kept my heart pure and have washed my hands in innocence. All day long I have been afflicted, and every morning brings new punishments. If I had spoken out like that, I would have betrayed your children. When I tried to understand all this, it troubled me deeply till I entered the sanctuary of God; then I understood their final destiny. Yet I am always with you; you hold me by my right hand.

You guide me with your counsel, and afterward you will take me into glory. Whom have I in heaven but you? And earth has nothing I desire besides you. My flesh and my heart may fail, but God is the strength of my heart and my portion forever. – Psalm 73 – Selected Verses

Dear Heavenly Father,

It's very easy for me to envy the wealthy carefree people around me that have no interest in you or living in repentance and faith. Sometimes you seem to bless them more than your struggling believers. It's comforting to know that a thousand years before your Son walked the earth that Asaph had the same inner struggle. And I love the solution you gave him. You are working in every life and we should never judge your justice until the end. That's when it all will make sense. I can live with your answer to wait because I know you gave up your Son for me. If you saved me like that, I know you can be trusted when you temporarily bless a godless person. Help me to see my own worldliness when I am chaffed by their success and help me to want them to experience grace and not justice. Make me a patient, loving friend instead of an envious judge. AMEN

Good grief is sadness over temporary loss. Bad grief is sadness without hope.

Additional Reading: 1 Kings 21 and 22

JULY 28

Jesus said to her, "I am the resurrection and the life. The one who believes in me will live, even though they die; and whoever lives by believing in me will never die. Do you believe this?" —John 11:25-26

Dear Jesus,
Yes, I believe what you told Martha that day at the grave of Lazarus. I believe that my dearest loved ones who have fallen asleep in the faith are still living with you, but sometimes I miss them so much that I cannot stop grieving for them. I need your help by your Holy Spirit to let your words be the thing that makes me happy that they are now happy with you. They are already living past the sad events surrounding their earthly end, but I get stuck reliving them. They are exploring new heights in heaven while I am running on the treadmill of loss and loneliness without them. I sometimes think that I am worried that we will forget them here. Maybe I am also afraid that they would forget me too. Oh, Jesus, your promise of a final and long-lasting reunion is my only hope. Thanks for the silver lining of redemption and heaven. Give me freedom from my grief so I can live well in my remaining days here before we are reunited in heaven.
AMEN

Grief shows the deep value of our personal relationships. Faith shows the deeper value of a Savior who really made all things new.

Additional Reading: 1 Corinthians 15, Job 19:23-27

JULY 29

Jesus fed over 5,000 people on the east side of the Lake of Galilee. Overnight he left with his disciples to the other side of the lake.

Once the crowd realized that neither Jesus nor his disciples were there, they got into the boats and went to Capernaum in search of Jesus. They found Jesus on the other side of the lake. Jesus told them, "Very truly I tell you, you are looking for me, not because you saw the signs, I performed but because you ate the loaves and had your fill. Do not work for food that spoils, but for food that endures to eternal life, which the Son of Man will give you. For on him God the Father has placed his seal of approval." —John 6:23-27

Dear Jesus,
I am so closely tied to the material world that I would have been just like those people. Once you bless me, I am right back at your feet begging for more food, more creature comforts, more temporal security. I love the tangible gifts you give to me more than the spiritual. It's hard to admit, but it is true. Help me to want you and the spiritual gift of eternal life more than the earthly things you freely give to me and my family. I believe you have already given me this gift that lasts. Help me to not just say it is meaningful to me. Instead make it my greatest treasure in the deepest place of my heart.
AMEN

God wants to be loved for the life he has given us n his Son more than the life he has given to us under his sun.

Additional Reading: 1 Corinthians 15:19-58

JULY 30

Our light and momentary troubles are achieving for us an eternal glory that far outweighs them all. – 2 Corinthians 4:17

Dear Jesus,
It is not normal to welcome disappointments and difficulties. It is not normal to believe that there really is good to come out of a relationship difficulty. No one I have ever met has told me that they like their health problems because ... So, when you say that all these "abnormal" things in my life are working something good for me, I have to listen in a concentrated way. Give me an open heart to genuinely see the spiritual and eternal benefit of all these so called "negatives." Give me the grace to believe that you are working great things into my life through the crosses you choose for me. Make me trust you from a heart that understands your greater good. And when I must attend the interment of one of my own earthly dreams, give me the strength not to erect a monument over its grave and obsess so much over the loss that I do not get on with the life the you have chosen for me.
AMEN

When you know heaven is waiting for you, you can patiently wait through great trials to get there.

Additional Reading: 2 Corinthians 4, Romans 8:12-30

JULY 31

The son said to him, "Father, I have sinned against heaven and against you. I am no longer worthy to be called your son." But the father said to his servants, "Quick! Bring the best robe and put it on him. Put a ring on his finger and sandals on his feet. Bring the fattened calf and kill it. Let's have a feast and celebrate. For this son of mine was dead and is alive again; he was lost and is found." So they began to celebrate. —Luke 15:21-24

Dear Jesus,
I love this parable that you told and I love this moment in the parable. The father's love for the son takes over the whole scene. It makes me realize that you and the Father are consumed with me as a child of yours rather than waiting to reject me when I fall. I am all too aware of my sins. It's your grace and love longing for my return that I often forget. Fill me with this grace and help me to live today as if I am in the same celebratory moment with you as this son was. You are throwing a party for me in your grace. Let's celebrate the salvation of my soul together!
AMEN

God wants us to rejoice as much as he does over the redemption that reconciles us to him.

Additional Reading: Luke 15

AUGUST 1

Therefore I urge you to imitate me. For this reason, I have sent to you Timothy, my son whom I love, who is faithful in the Lord. He will remind you of my way of life in Christ Jesus, which agrees with what I teach everywhere in every church. —1 Corinthians 4:16–17

Dear Jesus,
You have changed my life forever. Your love has rescued me, and your word has restored me. Now, I try to imitate you because I know you got it right in every circumstance. Help me to live like you so others can have a living 3D example of how you are when they watch me. I know I won't get it right all the time. But I am willing to be led to do better today. Give me an extra measure of your Spirit so I live a life way different than the world, all to your glory.
AMEN

Watching Jesus get life right with God makes us want to get off the bleachers and play on the same field of dreams.

Additional Reading: 2 Corinthians 3

AUGUST 2

When he saw the crowds he had compassion on them because they were harassed and helpless like sheep without a shepherd. Then he said to his disciples, "The harvest is plentiful but the workers are few. Ask the Lord of the harvest to send out more laborers into his harvest field."
– Matthew 9:30–33

Lord Jesus,
Yesterday I met two waitresses in a small town who were sponges for your word. They we're harassed by fear and trouble and they were confused about your word and promises. There are so many hungry people and so few dedicated to patiently explaining to them your love and truth. Please send out more people dedicated to teaching minds and leading hearts back home to you. And help me avoid useless and selfish distractions but to stay on the task of harvesting souls with my few remaining days. Help all your people to team up with their church to keep their lighthouse burning brightly.
Amen.

When we pray for more godly shepherds for people, we are kindred spirits with Jesus.

Additional Reading: 1 Timothy

AUGUST 3

"Love does not rejoice in evil but rejoices in the truth."
–1 Corinthians 13:6

Dear Lord Jesus,
In our culture this verse is particularly challenging. We are flooded with comedies on our televisions that showcase every kind of sexual innuendo and indiscretion that anyone could ever imagine, and we are trained to laugh. Dramas lead us to rejoice in revenge. It seems every station we click to is leading our hearts to indulge with a continual lust for the more absurd. Help me to find the "off" button and to prayerfully and honestly be happier with the truth about life, love, purity and faithfulness than the lie. Give me other things to do that bless and encourage my family and friends instead of wasting hours on questionable entertainment. I always feel better when I watch my intake as much as my outflow. Help me love the good and to neglect the seedier side of our culture. Thank you for giving me this desire. I know that it's you working in my heart.
AMEN

We must lead our hearts and not follow them.

Additional Reading: 1 John 3:1-3

AUGUST 4

If two lie down they can keep warm. But how can one keep warm alone?
—Ecclesiastes 4:11

Dear Lord,
You made us to live in constant contact and interdependence upon others. You want us striving and working together with the people you have placed in our lives. We need each other for help with basic needs and to meet the nuanced needs of our individual souls. We cannot "do life" alone. Thank you for the people you have given me that help me in ways beyond their own understanding. And give me the humility to let them help me "do life" in the best possible way. Help me to remember to express gratitude and encouragement also. I see your love and mercy in the people you have put on my team, especially my spouse and family. Thanks for being the great gracious God that you are.
AMEN

An attitude of gratitude is a mark of faith in the God of grace.

Additional Reading: Psalm 133, 1 Peter 1:22-2:2

AUGUST 5

Unless the Lord builds the house, the builders labor in vain. Unless the Lord watches over the city, the guards stand watch in vain. In vain you rise early and stay up late, toiling for food to eat— for he grants sleep to those he loves. Psalm 127:1-2

Dear Heavenly Father,
I love how you remind me that I do not have to work at life as if it all depended upon me. You are always at work and you are the captain of the ship. But I struggle to find the balance between working hard at my various callings and resting enough because I know that you are the big X factor. Help me to find joy in my work and family responsibilities as well as a peace in quiet reflective rest. In both work and rest, stay by my side and fill my soul with your grace. Without you I cannot do either.
AMEN

God has given us a lot of things to do but being anxious over any of them is not one of them.

Additional Reading: 2 Corinthians 8 and 9

AUGUST 6

So whether you eat or drink or whatever you do, do it all for the glory of God. —1 Corinthians 10:31

Dear Jesus,
It is so easy to create goals for myself that give me glory in their achievement. While I pursue them, they fill my life with meaning and purpose but once I have accomplished them, like an addict I am left empty and searching for a new goal. Help me to grasp the noble goal of simply glorifying you. Give me the power to break free from addiction to personal glory goals. Thank you for accomplishing so many goals for me that I can be content in just being loved by you. The contentment you grant is a huge blessing.
AMEN

Peace and contentment are the prize of faith.

Additional Reading: 1 Timothy 6:6-10

AUGUST 7

Therefore, do not be unwise, but understand what the will of the Lord is. And do not be drunk with wine, in which is dissipation; but be filled with the Spirit, speaking to one another in psalms and hymns and spiritual songs, singing and making melody in your heart to the Lord, giving thanks always for all things to God the Father in the name of our Lord Jesus Christ. –Ephesians 5:17-20

Dear Lord,
You have so much peace and tranquility to give your people every day. Help your church who is called by your name to find that peace which comes from singing hymns and spiritual songs in their hearts and with one another rather than from a bottle. When your saints self-medicate while claiming to live in the light of your freedom and grace it is a denial of the peace you promise to give freely to all who would trust your word enough to try using it to fill their hearts with your Spirit. Oh, God, help us to live the true spiritual life.
AMEN

Making melody in your heart to God will get you out of the blues.

Additional Reading: Galatians 5:13-26

AUGUST 8

If we claim to be without sin, we deceive ourselves and the truth is not in us. If we confess our sins, he is faithful and just and will forgive us our sins and purify us from all unrighteousness. If we claim we have not sinned, we make him out to be a liar and his word is not in us.
—1 John 1:8–9

Dear Jesus,
Your suffering on the cross has given me the courage to come out of the shadows of excuses and denial to face the ugliness of my own sins. I am the reason you hung there on that cross. But you are the reason too. You wanted to rescue me and get me out of my huge predicament. Now, help me to live the peaceful and honest life of one who is transparent about his failings and honest about his desire to get it right for your glory and other's good. I am so thankful that you forgive me each time I ask. It encourages me to keep coming back to you.
AMEN

When you live in the light of the SON you don't have to where sunscreen.

Additional Reading: Ephesians 4

AUGUST 9

Bear with each other and forgive one another if any of you has a grievance against someone. Forgive as the Lord forgave you. And over all these virtues put on love, which binds them all together in perfect unity.
—Colossians 3:13-14

Dear Jesus,
Help me and all those around me to live in the optimism caused by grace and forgiveness. I do not want to look at people as the ones who have disappointed me. Instead, I want to see them as precious souls that you have redeemed and have put in my life, so I can either introduce them to love and mercy or accent the love the mercy they already know. Come by your Holy Spirit and create in me the love that never dies for anyone and the mercy that binds me to them in peace. There is no unity like the unity that you create through your gospel in action.
AMEN

Don't make people feel like they live with a "speck inspector". Instead, help them find redeeming love wearing skin.

Additional Reading: 1 Corinthians 13

AUGUST 10

By faith Abraham, when God tested him, offered Isaac as a sacrifice. He who had embraced the promises was about to sacrifice his one and only son, even though God had said to him, "It is through Isaac that your offspring will be reckoned." Abraham reasoned that God could even raise the dead, and so in a manner of speaking he did receive Isaac back from death. —Hebrews 11:17–19

Dear Lord,
Abraham learned through the long saga of waiting for a child to trust your promises against all reason. Then you asked him to sacrifice his son for you. He stared at the unreasonableness of that request and still believed in your promise to keep Isaac on earth. He reasoned that you would raise him from the dead. He was wrong about that because you never let him kill Isaac. But he was right about trusting your promises. Help me to be "wrong and right" too. What I mean is that I am asking you to give me that faith that believes your word over all reason and that tolerates being left to contemplate just how you will fulfill each promise in my life. There's so much I don't know. But what I do know is that you will keep your promise to graciously bring me to a blessed end. Today, I will live by faith in you no matter how unpredictable the journey.
AMEN

Faith is a gift from God that enables you to properly use all his other gifts.

Additional Reading: Hebrews 11

AUGUST 11

When he had finished speaking, he said to Simon, "Put out into deep water, and let down the nets for a catch." Simon answered, "Master, we've worked hard all night and haven't caught anything. But because you say so, I will let down the nets." When they had done so, they caught such a large number of fish that their nets began to break.
—Luke 5:4-6

Dear Jesus,
I sometimes wonder why you keep my nets empty and watch me toil "all night" without any success. At those times I wonder if you are careless or cruel. But then you step in and orchestrate a windfall for me in the same area I was trying to work out my own solution and just like Peter I am overwhelmed with the thought that you are God and I am not. That's when the net in my heart is filled with faith and understanding. I look forward to empty nets if it means that I will ultimately get a full soul. Thank you for empty nets, because they set me up to learn anew that everything in my life really does depend totally on your blessing.
AMEN

Two foundational facts for human enlightenment: 1) There is a God! 2) You are not him.

Additional Reading: Ephesians 3:14-21

Donald W. Patterson

AUGUST 12

Do not work for food that spoils, but for food that endures to eternal life, which the Son of Man will give you. For on him God the Father has placed his seal of approval." Then they asked him, "What must we do to do the works God requires?" Jesus answered, "The work of God is this: to believe in the one he has sent." –John 6:27-29

Dear Lord Jesus,
When I read any of the words you spoke, they arrest my mind and make me think hard on revealing grace. There is nothing more antithetical to work than believing in someone else's work. So to say that the work that God the Father requires is to believe in you and your work, blows my mind. I was born believing in myself and really no one else. But you have taught me how wonderful it is to trade in that self-faith for faith in you and your wonderful forgiveness and acceptance. I do believe in you and the peace you have made for me on earth and in heaven. I work hard to live in that peace but help me when I struggle with my unbelief. When I am living immersed in your grace I feel confident, free to be myself and free to love others. Oh, Jesus do me and the others around me the favor of fastening me firmly in your grace again today.
AMEN

A leopard cannot change his spots, but nothing is impossible for God.

Additional Reading: Philippians 3

AUGUST 13

"Cast all your cares on him because he cares for you." –1 Peter 5:7

Dear Lord,
Sometimes I think I am all alone carrying the many concerns I have. I forget that you are near me and want me to give them to you. I see in Scripture how you often put people in impossible situations, so they would have to look for you to get your help. I think of the parting of the Red sea or the disciples in the boat during a squall on the Sea of Galilee. They had no choice but to let go of fear and beg you to be God for them. Well, I am begging you to be God for me. Fix those relationships. Take care of any legal entanglements. Protect my kids from the lost world that attracts their hearts from you. Help our church come together in grace and joy and to stay on mission for your name's sake and for the sake of the lost. Here, take all my concerns and be my God and Savior. And make me gentle since I don't have the stress of carrying everything alone anymore.
AMEN

We carry no needs by ourselves. So, don't act like you are all alone.

Additional Reading: Philippians 4:1-8

AUGUST 14

Rejoice in the Lord always. I will say it again: Rejoice! 5 Let your gentleness be evident to all. The Lord is near. 6 Do not be anxious about anything, but in every situation, by prayer and petition, with thanksgiving, present your requests to God. 7 And the peace of God, which transcends all understanding, will guard your hearts and your minds in Christ Jesus. —Philippians 4:4-7

Dear Jesus,
I love this passage because it gives me your divine plan for what I am to do with my stress. I can bring every problem to you and dump it off at your feet like your mother did at that the wedding of Cana in John 2. I do not have to helplessly mull over all the scenarios of how things might go for me and my loved ones. Instead, I can give it to you and let you handle it. Then I can be stress free, gentle and loving to all those around me. Thank you for teaching us through Paul the secret of spiritual stress management. It's a relationship with you, our loving and powerful Savior, who listens to our needs and promises to work out the best for us. Oh Jesus, guard my heart and mind from the ravages of worry!
Amen

God loves being God not just of the universe but also God of our vulnerable hearts.

Additional Reading: Matthew 6

AUGUST 15

I rejoiced with those who said to me, "Let us go to the house of the Lord." Our feet are standing in your gates, Jerusalem. – Psalm 122

Dear Lord,

I have been pondering why corporate worship is so important when each of us has an intense personal relationship with you. Then a brother wrote, "We need to gather with the church because we forget how desperate we are for redeeming grace, how complete are our resources in Christ, how God wants our spiritual life to be a group project, how life can never be found in the physical creation." In corporate worship, I am reminded that life is in you and not the passing world outside of the sanctuary. Help me to get myself to the gathering of believers so I may reap the benefits of the reorientation and restoration of my soul and may give others the same.
AMEN

Aloneness is good if we are alone with God and only for a time. Otherwise we need to be interlocking with the other pieces in God's jigsaw puzzle, so everyone can marvel at its collective beauty.

Additional Reading: Psalm 22:22-31, Hebrews 10:24-26

AUGUST 16

If you oh Lord kept a record of sins, who could stand. —Psalm 130:3

Dear Lord,
I catch myself thinking that I can stand in front of you because I do this or that well. Whenever I feel this way, I invariably catch myself thinking I am ahead of some other sinner in the "be good" game. And in my heart, I look down on them. But when I am alone with you, I cannot escape the painful truth that I often do not even want to do good. If you kept a record of my sins, I could not stand in front of you. That's why I love you so much. You have forgiven all my sins. There is no record of them to be found. I see only you and your accepting smile. Because you have forgotten my sins, I can forget them too.
AMEN

Forgiveness is God's supernatural power to make everything right in a wrong world.

Additional Reading: Psalm 103

AUGUST 17

Blessed be the God and Father of our Lord Jesus Christ. According to his great mercy, he has caused us to be born again into a living hope through the resurrection of Jesus Christ from the dead. –1 Peter 1:3

Dear Heavenly Father,
Having spent many hours, days and weeks, trying to secure a future for myself and others only to be surprised by sickness, troubles and the tentacles of death stealing away my loved ones, I find great peace and joy in your promise of a real future beyond this temporary "Olympic" struggle. You raised Christ from the dead to give me the same hope, my own resurrection to life. I accept your gift and I will let it give me hope today no matter what earthly disappointments and challenges I face. My hope is in you and my future is secure. Therefore, today is going to be a good day.
AMEN

God has already written the last chapter of our lives. It is a better end than we could ever imagine. So, smile through the large middle earth where you tread.

Additional Reading: 2 Corinthians 1

AUGUST 18

Love always protects. –1 Corinthians 13:7

Dear Lord,
I remember my father and mother protecting me against troubling influences that they saw creeping up around me when I was in my teens. They intervened and challenged me to walk with you and them in the right way. I understand more clearly today how much energy and effort it cost them. It's not easy to protect other people. It's hard and sometimes thankless work. But it is the true way to live. You say it simply, "Love protects." You perfectly protected your disciples and you have perfectly protected me. I take responsibility for venturing outside of that protection too often. Give me the desire and the ability to effectively protect those whom you have given to me to love.
AMEN

God chose whom we would love by planting them in the garden next to us. He will give us the strength to be their shade.

Additional Reading: Isaiah 32:1-8

AUGUST 19

I will marry you in faithfulness. Then you will know the Lord.
—Hosea 2:20

Dear Lord Jesus,
In divine love you married yourself to me knowing full well my wayward trends. You knew exactly what you were getting yourself into and you married me anyway. I am too often surprised by the weakness of those I choose to love. I struggle with a conditional heart. Oh, take away the taker in me. Make me a giver like you and I will help you change the world by your gospel love. In your name, I forgive everyone who has ever let me down and I chose to love them again with a heart charged with your unconditional grace and mercy.
Amen

We cannot receive love from God without being led to give love like God. His love never lies dormant in the soul.

Additional Reading: Revelation 21:1-6

AUGUST 20

We boast in the hope of the glory of God. —Romans 5:2

Dear Lord,
Most of the time we look back and find things to boast about. I like how you make us look forward to heaven in this verse. We haven't seen anything yet! What we will be and what we will get in heaven will be amazing. We will talk about it for centuries. Since we know that heaven is real, help us to live in hope. When I am tempted to look back at glory days, help me to be thankful but to remember that the best is yet to come. And Jesus, I glory in heaven for just one reason: you paid my ticket to fly there when all my earthly glory fades. Thanks for giving me a hope I cannot lose.
AMEN

Jesus has given us a hope that cannot be outshined by earthly glories or overwhelmed by earthly darkness.

Additional Reading: 2 Corinthians 4:16-5:10

AUGUST 21

Forgive as the Lord forgave you. —Colossians 3:13

Dear Lord Jesus,
It's perhaps the greatest example of how far humanity fell in the beginning, that we struggle to forgive. And you talk about it all over your book and it was the only part of the Lord's Prayer about which you expanded afterward. With forgiveness you challenged your disciples and with forgiveness you test us to see whether we are in the faith. I know that forgiveness is the hardest virtue for me to practice and I sense that others have a hard time forgiving me too. Oh, Jesus, fill us with your redeeming grace and help us forgive each other from the heart.
AMEN

Life is too short to be squandered in un-forgiveness.

Additional Reading: Genesis 50, Psalm 130

AUGUST 22

Beloved, I pray that in all respects you may prosper and be in good health, just as your soul prospers. —3 John 2.

Dear Jesus,
I love this verse because it teaches me to pray for my friends and family more than engage them. Please help me not to make every flaw I see in one of them as a challenge for me to "fix" them. I will give my observations and concerns to you and trust how you will work your miracles in their hearts and lives. And when you want me to say a timely word to them, please make it obvious to me and give me the courage and love to say it well. Now, having prayed this; I will relax and serve you with a cheerful heart today.
AMEN

The triangle between God and one of his children praying for another is a strong spiritual shape.

Additional Reading: Philippians 1

AUGUST 23

So, in Christ Jesus you are all children of God through faith, for all of you who were baptized into Christ have clothed yourselves with Christ. There is neither Jew nor Gentile, neither slave nor free, nor is there male and female, for you are all one in Christ Jesus. If you belong to Christ, then you are Abraham's seed, and heirs according to the promise. –Galatians 3:26-29

Dear Jesus,

I love how you have released me from looking at myself as a winner or loser at anything. I am your child, chosen to play on your team and all my other Christian friends are the same. No one wins or loses without the other. I look at myself and them totally different when they are wearing your jersey. When they fall, they take me with them. When they succeed, they lift me up to the platform to share in their glory. We are all one in you. Because you are our best teammate as the player/coach, we all cash in on your victory. Thank you for putting me on your team. Help me to accept and love my teammates and to play my position well. AMEN

Wisdom is learning to accept and play along with those teammates that God has chosen to be with us on his team.

Additional Reading: 1 Corinthians 12

AUGUST 25

Jesus wept. —John 11:35

Dear Jesus,
You wept deeply at the grave of your friend, Lazarus. You feel all our pain from every experience. You know what it feels like to be trapped in this world where loss is the order of things. Thank you for not only winning for us a way out but for doing it by entering our entire grieving experience. You are the God who knows and cares. It makes me feel not so alone as I struggle to hang onto the gospel knot in my rope.
AMEN

God knows. God cares. God rescues.

Additional Reading: 2 Corinthians 1, 1 Peter 5:7-11

AUGUST 26

Whatever you do, do it enthusiastically, as something done for the Lord and not for men. —Colossians 3:23

Dear Lord Jesus,

This verse gives me a much better reason to do my best and with a good heart than I can usually think of myself. I tend to need the affirmation of people in order to get excited about doing something. Or I need to believe there is some hope for success by my standards. And if someone gives me the least criticism, I tend to get a flat tire in my heart. But when I do what I do for you, ah, then there is a resilient reason to do it. You are always seeking my good. You promise to bring good out of my "bad". I can have hope of true success and will always know that your correction comes from a good heart. Today, I will live my life enthusiastically for you. After all, you lived yours enthusiastically for me and you still enthusiastically pursue me every day.
AMEN

When we live for the Lord we will live boldly in calm and in strife.

Additional Reading: 1 Corinthians 4:1-5

AUGUST 27

But the wisdom that comes from heaven is first pure; then peace-loving, considerate, submissive, full of mercy and good fruit, impartial and sincere. —James 3:17

Dear Jesus,
I know that I must have serious communication and even conflict with people on some occasions. It seems inevitable that in order to uphold the truth I will collide with people. But I want to reflect the gentleness and respect that come from love when I must stand up for the truth or stand down someone who is wrong. I want to disagree with dignity and speak with a merciful tone. Please give me your supernatural ability to build bridges when I must enter conflict instead of burning bridges down.
AMEN

The Christ within us wins people before arguments.

Additional Reading: 1 Corinthians 13

AUGUST 28

Do not merely look out for your own interests but also for the interests of others. – Philippians 2:4

Dear Lord,
I too easily filter everything I hear through my own perspective. I want to put others first and their interests in front of mine. Help me to see every choice that I make with family or friends as an opportunity to serve them and help them find happiness during their short journey on earth. Make me give in where I can without compromising truth. Keep me from mistaking my own opinion for your unchangeable truth. Get rid of stubbornness that makes me insist I have my schedule my own way. Help me find joy in giving and in giving in. All of this will take miraculous power on your part. But I believe you can do it in me. If you did not spare your Son to save me, you can easily change my obdurate heart.
AMEN

There is nothing so sweet as being released from slavery to self.

Additional Reading: Mark 10:35-45

AUGUST 29

Husbands ought to love their wives as their own bodies,
—Ephesians 5:28

Dear Heavenly Father,
You gave my spouse to me in order to complete me. Help me not to forget that she is as much a part of me as my right hand. When she is hurt give me the concern for her that I have for an injured limb. Help me to cherish her and take care of her and to give her the best opportunity to shine. And thank you for giving her to me as a best friend. Help me to remember that she is my friend when she gently reproves me for my mistakes that anyone close to me is bound to see. Help both of us to live in grace for one another and not in a plethora of little rules. For all those who do not have spouses, give them one or two very close friends with whom they can share their deeper thoughts and emotions, dreams and challenges, fears and triumphs.
AMEN

A spouse is not a family car that you replace when you get tired of it. He/she is an integral part of your own body and soul the second you say, 'I do.'

Additional Reading: Ephesians 5:21-33

AUGUST 30

In all this you greatly rejoice, though now for a little while you may have had to suffer grief in all kinds of trials. These have come so that the proven genuineness of your faith—of greater worth than gold, which perishes even though refined by fire—may result in praise, glory and honor when Jesus Christ is revealed. –1 Peter 1:6-7

Dear Jesus,
I now know that you are not working to deliver to me my own personal definition of happiness. You are working to change me into the image of your perfect son, who loved you and all people perfectly, who trusted you without flaw and could be trusted by every person. Your agenda is to make me into a new person. My agenda has been for you to make me a new life on earth that has no suffering. I know heaven is that place where no one suffers. I don't belong there yet. I belong here in my present suffering in order to learn, grow and bless others who are on the same journey. Make me a wise pilgrim who travels and learns how to follow you. And thank you for redeeming me through the journey of suffering that your own Son took.
AMEN

God does not intend for our lives to be easy. He intends for them to be challenging training grounds where he changes us from what we are to what he always intended us to be.

Additional Reading: Romans 8:12-39

AUGUST 31

Whoever dwells in the shelter of the Most High will rest in the shadow of the Almighty. — Psalm 91:1

Dear Heavenly Father,
Sometimes I feel so vulnerable to the whims of disease or threats of bad weather or the undiscerned thoughts of crazy people. It seems I must always be alert, or I will not survive. Then I read that I can find shelter in you. Hide me in the shadow of your wings. Be my protector from everything that can harm me or those I love. Free me from worry so that I can spend my energy and strength building others up in the faith rather than trying to circle the wagons to protect myself.
AMEN

Worry is taking responsibility for things that God takes care of.

Additional Reading: Matthew 6:25-34

SEPTEMBER 1

Those who live according to the Spirit set their minds on what the Spirit desires. Romans 8:5

Dear Holy Spirit,
Help me to want what you want and to do what you do. I am weary if having my own way. When I want what you want I will desire to be good without fear or frustration. Fill me with that desire.
Amen

It's much more fulfilling to follow the Holy Spirit than to follow yourself.

Additional Reading: Galatians 5 and 6

SEPTEMBER 1

I lift up my eyes to the mountains — where does my help come from? My help comes from the Lord, the Maker of heaven and earth.
—Psalm 121:1-2

Dear Lord,
You have given me many strengths and talents and have taught me to faithfully use them to take care of my family and me. I have enjoyed great freedoms and independence in a country that you provided that gives me great opportunities. My life is free and fun in this corner of your world. But I increasingly realize how much you have done to provide the scene, deliver the opportunities and bless my efforts. I am also keenly aware that I need you for help in every area of my life. Your supernatural grip on the entire universe and your specific intervention in my personal affairs is what allows me to survive and thrive. I look to you for help. I put my life into your loving hands today.
Amen

God's hands hold us in life and hug us in the next.

Additional Reading: Luke 12:4-7

SEPTEMBER 2

In the first place, I hear that when you come together as a church, there are divisions among you, and to some extent I believe it. No doubt there have to be differences among you to show which of you have God's approval. –1 Corinthians 11:18–19

Dear Jesus,
This passage has both comforted and confronted me since the day I met it. During his diatribe against arguing, Paul admitted that church debates do have some virtue. They reveal who is really walking by truth, faith and love. I wonder every time I'm caught in a conflict whether you see me acting in truth and love or selfish ambition and stubbornness. It makes me stop and think, evaluate and then pray. Thank you so much for this verse. It changes everything about the debates that encircle me. And it reminds me of your stabilizing presence and oversight in every situation.
AMEN

Winning the argument is not near as important as loving God and your adversary in the fray.

Additional Reading: Romans 12

SEPTEMBER 3

Do not let any unwholesome talk come out of your mouths, but only what is helpful for building others up according to their needs, that it may benefit those who listen. 30 And do not grieve the Holy Spirit of God, with whom you were sealed for the day of redemption. 31 Get rid of all bitterness, rage and anger, brawling and slander, along with every form of malice. 32 Be kind and compassionate to one another, forgiving each other, just as in Christ God forgave you.
—Ephesians 4:29-32

Dear Jesus,
Put a sentry at the door of my mouth that makes me think hard about everything I say so that all words are soft and gentle even when they are pointed and forthright. Give me a forgiving heart like yours so I'm reticent to remind people of their failings just to change behavior or get my way. Help me get rid of all arguments and debate and make all my words build faith and share truth. Help me speak words worth remembering that no one tries to forget.
Amen

We do more with our mouths whether good or bad than we do with our hands and feet.

Additional Reading: James 3

SEPTEMBER 4

Therefore I tell you, do not worry about your life, what you will eat; or about your body, what you will wear. For life is more than food, and the body more than clothes. Consider the ravens: They do not sow or reap, they have no storeroom or barn; yet God feeds them. And how much more valuable you are than birds! Who of you by worrying can add a single hour to your life? Since you cannot do this very little thing, why do you worry about the rest? – Luke 12:22-26

Lord Jesus,

You ask me why I worry about my money, my possessions, my health and my life? It is because I easily fall into the temptation that it all depends on me. I cannot see you and hear your voice. But the bills keep coming. The doctor's reports are real hard data. My AC still breaks, and my transmission goes out costing me unexpected 1000's. I still have relationship challenges, no, I mean problems. The birds live with all kinds of challenges too, but they cannot think ahead like I can. They just live for today. I get your truth; you take care of us both. The birds cannot see or hear you either, but they don't worry and enjoy their lives more than I do. My problem is that I know too much, and I think too much. But it is also that I know too little and think too little–I think too little about your love, your promises to provide, your absolute control of all things. Help me to live in the peace that you are taking care of me and mine so that I live in joy as a bright light of what you can do when you free a heart from worry.
AMEN

God will take care of you. So, care less about everything.

Additional Reading: 2 Corinthians 9

SEPTEMBER 5

Jacob stole his brother's blessing and then ran for his life. This is what happened next: "Jacob had a dream in which he saw a stairway resting on the earth, with its top reaching to heaven, and the angels of God were ascending and descending on it. There above it stood the Lord, and he said: "I am the Lord, the God of your father Abraham and the God of Isaac. I will give you and your descendants the land on which you are lying. Your descendants will be like the dust of the earth, and you will spread out to the west and to the east, to the north and to the south. All peoples on earth will be blessed through you and your offspring. I am with you and will watch over you wherever you go, and I will bring you back to this land. I will not leave you until I have done what I have promised you. – Genesis 28:12-15

Dear God,
Who are you that you would give such pure unilateral promises to such a scoundrel like Jacob. Why was there no scolding, no threats if he did not change, no "time outs"? Who are you that you bless a sinner like him with such profound gifts in this life, in history and in heaven? How do you expect us to respect your justice when you freely forgive and bless a guy like that? Your prodigal love is too much to process. If I were God, do you know what I would do? I would …. I would … uh …. I would make a mess out of everything because I would eventually judge all people to hell including myself. Oh, God, you are the most incredible God of grace, who keeps his promises when we are not keeping ours. I will let you be God and I will let you love me and the other stinkers around me. I plead with you, make us as gracious and constant as you are. Restore our relationships and renew our hearts in your purposeful life changing love.
AMEN

There is no power like God's love given freely to my heart when I least deserve it.

Additional Readings: 1 John 4 and 5

SEPTEMBER 6

May the God who gives endurance and encouragement give you the same attitude of mind toward each other that Christ Jesus had, so that with one mind and one voice you may glorify the God and Father of our Lord Jesus Christ. – Romans 15:5

Dear God,
I love how this verse calls you the God of endurance. You are the one who endures through all of time, through all sinner's foibles, through the wickedness and the good of all humanity – as each generation passes you remain back and keep plugging along with a new one. I, on the other hand easily quit and take breaks from serving. Thank you for enduring for me. I remember when I was a child how if my father or mother would help me with anything, I seemed to have renewed endurance. Please come and help me today so that I endure my situations with strong faith and love because I know you are there helping me.
AMEN

God calls you to persevere by faith and he stays right there with you to give you the help you need.

Additional Readings: Matthew 28, Revelation 1:9-20

SEPTEMBER 7

*Even youths grow tired and weary,
and young men stumble and fall;
but those who hope in the Lord
will renew their strength.
They will soar on wings like eagles;
they will run and not grow weary,
they will walk and not be faint. – Isaiah 40:30–31*

Dear Lord,
I am tired of living as if it all depends on me. You made me and you sustain me. You also can give me strength to face all my challenges with a brave heart. Renew my strength today so by your help I will be able to meet my responsibilities with confidence and peace. I want to be there for my family and friends, and I want to do good things in your name. Come and be the wind beneath my wings.

When God lifts you up, you will fly above your weaknesses and troubles.

Additional Readings: 2 Corinthians 12:9

SEPTEMBER 8

He said to them, "How foolish you are, and how slow to believe all that the prophets have spoken! Did not the Messiah have to suffer these things and then enter his glory?" And beginning with Moses and all the Prophets, he explained to them what was said in all the Scriptures concerning himself. They asked each other, "Were not our hearts burning within us while he talked with us on the road and opened the Scriptures to us?" - Luke 24:25-27, 32

Dear Jesus,
As the resurrected Lord you gently chided your disciples for being depressed and then opened the Scriptures to them so they could see that your living word had promised all your suffering would end with resurrection to life. Their hearts burned with joy as they learned from you. My heart burns with joy too. Every year Easter brings my life into sharp perspective. I am saved. I am loved. I am going to live past the death experience and my body will be reborn without fault in the resurrection on the last day. This gives me sure hope to live by. How can I live with dead end thoughts about my life when I know what happened at Easter? Make your Easter message last in my heart for the rest of my life. You are risen and I will live forever. Thank you for patiently teaching and re-teaching me the reality of salvation.
AMEN

In Christ we have a sure hope that gives us a lifetime of "Spring-like "optimism.

Additional Readings: Romans 1

SEPTEMBER 9

And he took bread, gave thanks and broke it, and gave it to them, saying, "This is my body given for you; do this in remembrance of me."
– Luke 22:19

Dear Jesus,
We all want to be remembered after we are gone. But when I think about it, I want to be remembered for selfish reasons. I am insecure about my life and want to know that I was significant enough to be remembered. But you gave us this great supper, so we would remember you for our own benefit. How easily we forget that our spiritual connection is totally dependent on your sacrifice and grace. With this regular meal we are drawn back to redeeming grace and our appreciation of your undying love is rekindled and then we believe in divine love again. What an ingenious gift you left for us – a tangible way to remember grace! Thank you for Maundy Thursday and what it gives all of us.
AMEN

The Lord's Supper is made with love, for love and to love.

Additional Reading: 1 Corinthians 11

SEPTEMBER 10

"When Jesus said this, one of the officials nearby slapped him in the face. "Is this the way you answer the high priest?" he demanded. "If I said something wrong," Jesus replied, "testify as to what is wrong. But if I spoke the truth, why did you strike me?" – John 18:22-23

Dear Jesus,
On this day of all days, you endured three trials. The first was in the wee hours of the morning, before Annas who was no longer the high priest. When you tried to get him and his friends to see the error of their ways, they struck you. And you asked why? "Why did you strike me?"—I know why he struck you. It was the hand of justice against my sin that struck you all day long until you shouted, "It is finished." You had to go this road alone. None of us could walk it for you or for us; You alone saved me. And for that I owe you my love and my heart. The only good that came out of that day was the only good that will last forever for me – I am redeemed. Thank you, Lord Jesus. Help me reflect my love for you by giving me the strength to absorb the sins of others the way you have mine.
AMEN

"On this day, he did it all."

Additional Readings: Zechariah 3:1-10

Donald W. Patterson

SEPTEMBER 11

"We fix our eyes on Jesus, the pioneer and perfecter of faith. For the joy set before him he endured the cross, scorning its shame, and sat down at the right hand of the throne of God. 3 Consider him who endured such opposition from sinners, so that you will not grow weary and lose heart." – Hebrews 12:2-3

Dear Jesus,
On this day in your final week you rested quietly out at Bethany. Oh, how that day must have been filled with contemplation of the betrayal of a friend, the denial of your chosen leader and the filthy hate that would be heaped upon you by lost souls. But I am guessing that what the passage says above was also there; for the joy set before you of redeeming me you were comforted and peacefully happy. That blows my mind. But it also fills my soul with hope in the joy of heaven with you. I may suffer but I have a joy that stands beyond the darkness. I will run the race because I know you are there at the end smiling with a redeeming grin.
AMEN

"I can face my life today because I will be with Christ tomorrow."

Additional Reading: 2 Timothy 1:3-14

SEPTEMBER 12

Early in the morning, as Jesus was on his way back to the city, he was hungry. 19 Seeing a fig tree by the road, he went up to it but found nothing on it except leaves. Then he said to it, "May you never bear fruit again!" Immediately the tree withered.
20 When the disciples saw this, they were amazed. "How did the fig tree wither so quickly?" they asked.
21 Jesus replied, "Truly I tell you, if you have faith and do not doubt, not only can you do what was done to the fig tree, but also you can say to this mountain, 'Go, throw yourself into the sea,' and it will be done. 22 If you believe, you will receive whatever you ask for in prayer." – Matthew 21:18-22

Dear Jesus,
On Monday of that last week of your life you went into Jerusalem and cleansed the temple of busyness and restored it to a spiritual house of prayer and godly teaching. You cursed a fig tree for not producing the fruit it was supposed to and so showed all of us with that illustration that you and your Father created us to produce spiritual fruit of love, faith and hope. Oh Jesus, rescue me from business about so many temporal things that I do not produce true spiritual insight, faith, hope and love for myself or anyone else. Open my heart and cleanse it of frenetic activity that dulls spiritual sensitivity and maturity. Give me the peace and strength to sit quietly and meditate on your word and you love and what it means for my life and the lives of those in my family and among my friends.
Amen

Think more about what Christ has done for you than you do about what you are doing for him.

Additional Reading: Colossians 2

Donald W. Patterson

SEPTEMBER 13

They arrived again in Jerusalem, and while Jesus was walking in the temple courts, the chief priests, the teachers of the law and the elders came to him. "By what authority are you doing these things?" they asked. "And who gave you authority to do this?" – Mark 11:27-28

Jesus,
When you cleansed the temple on that holy Monday so many years ago, the leaders of visible Israel were enraged. You had upset their little kingdom that they thought was dedicated to your Father but blindly it had been a religious world that had themselves at the center. You knocked them off the throne and they hated it. We always at first hate it when you do that to us. You come into our circumstances and change everything, and it makes us cry out for answers. "What gives you authority to run my life instead of me?" Oh, Jesus, I want my life to be a temple dedicated to you and not my own plans and dreams. I know by what authority you have come and changed things for me – it is by the authority of your love. Your love for me drives you to knock me off my feet so you can pick me up and carry me. Lord Jesus, carry me through all my present struggles and cleanse my temple anytime it needs it.
AMEN

God knocks us down from our self-sufficiency so he can pick us up and carry us.

Additional Reading: Romans 3

SEPTEMBER 14

By faith Joseph, when his end was near, spoke about the exodus of the Israelites from Egypt and gave instructions concerning the burial of his bones. – Hebrews 11:22

Dear Heavenly Father,
What great wisdom you gave Joseph that he would make his people keep up with his bones for hundreds of years until you fulfilled your promise to send them back to the promised land. As each generation told the next about the bones they also told them about your promises. It's your promises that produce faith in us. Thank you for giving me parents who passed on your promises to me. When my heart was still wet cement they carefully made sure I knew all the big and wonderful promises that I hang my faith on. Help me to pass along your promises to my children and grandchildren. Give me creative ways to help them remember you are their God, you have redeemed them, that you are there for them and that you will welcome them into glory.
Amen

Family leadership is passing the baton of God's promises from one generation to the next.

Additional Reading: Psalm 78

SEPTEMBER 15

"If the Spirit of him who raised Jesus from the dead is living in you, he who raised Christ from the dead will also give life to your mortal bodies because of his Spirit who lives in you." – Romans 8:11

Dear Lord,
Every day I try to do well in serving you. I know you like to see me try. But you also know how I fall short. I am thankful that you forgive and don't dwell on my shortcomings. I don't want to dwell on them either. But I have a request, by your Spirit who lives in me, help me get it right more often for my good and your glory. By your Spirit change my desires. Give me keen discernment. Make me see exactly what is going on around me and help me figure out what to do about the complicated messes that get thrown at me. I want to press redeeming grace into the corner of the world around me. I need you every minute of today to do this. So, walk with me and give spiritual life to this dead head.
AMEN

If it were not for air, I'd be gone. If it were not for God's Spirit I would be the walking dead.

Additional Reading: John 6:60-69

SEPTEMBER 16

"All things have been created through him and for him."
— Colossians 1:16

Dear Lord Jesus,
I know I do it every day. I wake up and act like all things have been created for me. This basic attitude is the source of all my self-made dreams, my irritations and my conflicts. I naturally think the world revolves around me. As stuck as I am, I am also ashamed of being this way. I am thankful for the sake of everyone else that I am wrong too. All things were created through you and for you. And you are the only One to be trusted with them all. You make all things work out for everyone's good. So, I step into your world today, for your purposes to accomplish your dreams. It feels so much better to serve your much bigger plan than it does to serve myself. Thank you for rescuing me by your grace and resetting my dials.
AMEN

It is much more peaceful and satisfying to serve God than it is to serve ourselves.

Additional Reading: Romans 14

SEPTEMBER 16

And what more shall I say? I do not have time to tell about Gideon, Barak, Samson and Jephthah, about David and Samuel and the prophets, 33 who through faith conquered kingdoms, administered justice, and gained what was promised; who shut the mouths of lions, 34 quenched the fury of the flames, and escaped the edge of the sword; whose weakness was turned to strength; and who became powerful in battle and routed foreign armies. 35 Women received back their dead, raised to life again. There were others who were tortured, refusing to be released so that they might gain an even better resurrection. 36 Some faced jeers and flogging, and even chains and imprisonment. 37 They were put to death by stoning; they were sawed in two; they were killed by the sword. They went about in sheepskins and goatskins, destitute, persecuted and mistreated — 38 the world was not worthy of them. They wandered in deserts and mountains, living in caves and in holes in the ground. 39 These were all commended for their faith, yet none of them received what had been promised, 40 since God had planned something better for us so that only together with us would they be made perfect.
– Hebrews 11:32-40

Dear Jesus,
Your list of Old Testament saints that endured terrible persecutions in this world is very humbling to me. The endured the loss of everything, even their lives for the sake of their faith in you. I on the other hand live in a country that protects my religious freedom, allows me to spread and defends my human rights. Thank you for the blessings of my country and give me the faith and love to use this freedom to lead others to you instead of fritter away my time on only selfish pleasures. Drive the lukewarmness out of my heart and kindle in me a fire that cannot be quenched.
Amen

Freedom brings with it the responsibility to shine.

Additional Reading: Revelation 3:14-22

SEPTEMBER 17

"I am the good shepherd; I know my sheep and my sheep know me."
– John 10:14

Dear Jesus,
Too often I feel alone with my thoughts and emotions just wandering through life looking for pasture. But I feel the most loved and settled and at peace when I fix my thoughts on you and think hard about your words and what they mean for me personally. I can tell when people speak whether their thoughts are in line with your words. Your words are simple, clear truth and they comfort me. They give truth and they give grace. You are the good shepherd of my soul. I am not a wandering sheep. I am a lamb in your pasture. I will feed on your words and I will work hard at not needing any other approval other than what you gave at your cross for me.
AMEN

There is nothing more peaceful than believing that you are perfectly known and yet dearly loved by God.

Additional Reading: Psalm 23

SEPTEMBER 18

"You keep him in perfect peace whose mind is stayed on you, because he trusts in you." – Isaiah 26:3

Dear God,
There is so much I do not understand about my life. I have thrown all my theology at it, I have thrown all of my experience at it and nothing sticks. Some things just can't be filtered through. I am learning to trust you not because of great insights and emotional breakthroughs but just because you promise to make everything new. Today, I am going to take a vacation from trying to link my faith to my understanding of the meaning of my life apart from being redeemed. It is enough to be your child and to have the promise of being with you in person, forever. The rest can go out with the trash and it won't change my destiny. My mind is stayed on you. Please, free me from my lust for sorting out the details as if I must know how each piece fits in order to be at peace.
AMEN

We don't trust God because he makes perfect sense to us. We trust him because he is God and we are not.

Additional Reading: Philippians 4:4-9

SEPTEMBER 19

I always thank my God as I remember you in my prayers, because I hear about your love for all his holy people and your faith in the Lord Jesus. – Philemon 4-5

Dear Lord,
Today I pray for your bride, the church. I see so many of your saints who are either indifferent or critical of their brothers and sisters in the faith and they are starving each other of the unending grace that you gave us to enjoy as the wealth of our faith. Somehow, they think they are offering you service by rejecting fellow Christians over matters that have nothing to do with truth. Oh, Jesus, fill us with your loving Holy Spirit so we fulfill your deep desire to see us love one another the way that Paul encouraged Philemon. If we must spar about matters that need resolution, help us to fight more like friends having a pillow fight rather than enemies shooting high powered rifles at one another.
AMEN

A godly person will show you love even when they are sharply disagreeing with you.

Additional Reading: Philippians 1

SEPTEMBER 20

Not that I have already obtained all this, or have already arrived at my goal, but I press on to take hold of that for which Christ Jesus took hold of me. 13 Brothers and sisters, I do not consider myself yet to have taken hold of it. But one thing I do: Forgetting what is behind and straining toward what is ahead, 14 I press on toward the goal to win the prize for which God has called me heavenward in Christ Jesus.
– Philippians 3:12–14

Dear Jesus,
You have freed me from my past, even up to the last hour when I failed you. I no longer need to be paralyzed by guilt and shame over my sins. I'm free to look ahead without concern about my past catching up with me. Instead, I'm bold to love those I have hurt by being honest and apologetic when I see them. I'm bold to love those who are difficult to love because I know you will change their future through my love. I can have amnesia about all things behind me and simply focus on loving you and people. What a joy filled life this is! You really do give me life to the full.
Amen

When you want to go back and relive your mistakes, picture Jesus standing in the way saying, "Turn around and enjoy your future."

Additional Reading: John 10

SEPTEMBER 21

May the God who gives endurance and encouragement give you the same attitude of mind toward each other that Christ Jesus had, so that with one mind and one voice you may glorify the God and Father of our Lord Jesus Christ. – Romans 15:5-6

Dear Heavenly Father,
I sometimes get so weary of enduring life in my situation and with the people you have wedged me between. I know they get weary of enduring me too. I am even less enduring with my worldly generation that is rushing headlong into hedonism and selfishness. But you are the God who gives endurance and I need a heavy dose from you now. Please give me the encouragement that I need to take one more step and complete one more day of service to you and them. Make me an instrument of your peace and unity. Help me to make the most abrasive soul feel loved and connected. I will not have to endure this forever, but you will still be here enduring people after my departure to your glory in heaven. So, reach down into your storehouse of love and pour it on me so I can finish this race.
AMEN

I don't want to win. I just want to finish as a friend of God.

Additional Reading: Colossians 3

SEPTEMBER 22

For, as I have often told you before and now tell you again even with tears, many live as enemies of the cross of Christ. 19 Their destiny is destruction, their god is their stomach, and their glory is in their shame. Their mind is set on earthly things. 20 But our citizenship is in heaven. And we eagerly await a Savior from there, the Lord Jesus Christ, 21 who, by the power that enables him to bring everything under his control, will transform our lowly bodies so that they will be like his glorious body. – Philippians 3:18–21

Dear Jesus,
I'm in a constant battle within to not let my life be about things, places, entertainment and pleasure. These all perish with the using. They are blessings in life but like icing on a cake or cotton candy their sweetness soon fades and sometimes they even put unwanted weight on my life. Give me the divine perspective that guides me to gratefully use the blessings in my life for the betterment of others and myself so we both live by faith for heaven. Also, give me spiritual eyes to see earthly setbacks and failures as creative blessings from your hand. Fill me with hope that laughs at disappointments because of your promises to work good behind them for the greatest blessings forever.
Amen

We cannot know yet what great things God has in store for us, but we know it's got to be good if he sacrificed his own Son so that we could be there to get them.

Additional Reading: Romans 8 and 12

SEPTEMBER 23

How Long Lord? Will you forget me forever? How long will you hide your face from me? How long must I wrestle with my thoughts and day after day have sorrow in my heart? How long will my enemy triumph over me? – Psalm 13:1-2

Dear heavenly Father,
I can feel all alone when I'm suffering from health problems or some situation outside of my control. I pray and pray and never here a sound from you. I know you love me along with everyone else, but I still often feel it would be more loving for your to audibly comfort and guide me. It's comforting to meet David in this psalm and see he had the same frustration while suffering. You promise to speak to my soul through your word. Help me find your voice there and to trust your unfailing love no matter how long I must wait for answers or rescue. I trust you as my Savior and I will wait patiently for your help and rescue.
Amen

God is worthy of our love and trust even when we cannot make any sense out of our lives under his heaven.

Additional Reading: Psalm 73

SEPTEMBER 24

Seek the Lord while he may be found; call on him while he is near with the wicked forsake their ways and the unrighteous their thoughts. Let them turn to the Lord and he will have mercy on them and to our God for he will freely pardon. — Isaiah 55:6-7

Dear Lord,
You are quick to forgive even when you must let us endure the consequences of our actions as discipline. Your grace makes me quicker to return to you in apology. Help me to trust that if I share your forgiveness with people, they will have the courage to repent also. You are the God who pardons. Make me the Christian who tells sinners the truth about your prodigal love.

The grace of God gives us hope enough to turn ourselves in before his throne.

Additional Reading: 1 John 1:8-9

SEPTEMBER 25

For by the grace given me I say to every one of you: Do not think of yourself more highly than you ought, but rather think of yourself with sober judgment, in accordance with the faith God has distributed to each of you. For just as each of us has one body with many members, and these members do not all have the same function, so in Christ we, though many, form one body, and each member belongs to all the others. – Romans 12:3–5

Dear God,
In this word from Paul I see two ditches in which I can fall. On the one hand I can think that I am so gifted that I can do more than the rest and so I will try to control every task in the family or the church. I could think I am just too smart to not exert my influence and help. But on the other hand, I could believe that I am so below average in my gifts that I do not believe I have the need to offer any help in important matters. Instead, I will think I have permission to waste valuable time entertaining myself and playing through life. Either ditch is foolish thinking and it keeps from living in the truth. I see that you have gifted me with some gifts for the good of others and have also given them some gifts for my benefit. I want to fit together happily with each one. Help me to accept my gifts and responsibly to serve others while I also graciously let them serve and shine with their gifts.
AMEN

Be who you are and not more or less. Then you will enjoy the ride God designed for you.

Additional Reading: 1 Peter 4, 1 Corinthians 12

SEPTEMBER 26

We know that the law is spiritual; but I am unspiritual, sold as a slave to sin. I do not understand what I do. For what I want to do I do not do, but what I hate I do. And if I do what I do not want to do, I agree that the law is good. As it is, it is no longer I myself who do it, but it is sin living in me. For I know that good itself does not dwell in me, that is, in my sinful nature. For I have the desire to do what is good, but I cannot carry it out. For I do not do the good I want to do, but the evil I do not want to do—this I keep on doing. Now if I do what I do not want to do, it is no longer I who do it, but it is sin living in me that does it. So, I find this law at work: Although I want to do good, evil is right there with me. For in my inner being I delight in God's law; but I see another law at work in me, waging war against the law of my mind and making me a prisoner of the law of sin at work within me. What a wretched man I am! Who will rescue me from this body that is subject to death? Thanks be to God, who delivers me through Jesus Christ our Lord! — Romans 7:14-25

Dear Lord Jesus,

I look forward to many things in heaven but none so much as the freedom I will experience from my sinful self. I am so tired of knowing the right thing to think and do but choosing to do the wrong. The more I learn about your will and ways, the more it feels like there are signs everywhere saying, "Wet paint" just begging me to touch. I can see from a distance a negative reaction to a problem and promise myself that I will not do it, and almost like the script of a predictable movie, there I go, thinking and saying the very thing I promised you and me both that I would not! I can't stand me! But I'm glad that you can. You rescue me with grace first and grace last. I am forgiven. I am loved. I am strengthened. I know that I can improve with your grace and power, but improvement is not what I need as much as grace. Help me always to desire both but to live in grace while I simply work on improvement. I want to keep in step with your Spirit. AMEN

Being a child of God is much better than doing everything perfectly.

Additional Reading: 1 John 2:19-24

SEPTEMBER 27

Are not five sparrows sold for two pennies? And not one of them is forgotten before God. Why, even the hairs of your head are all numbered. Fear not; you are of more value than many sparrows.
—Luke 12:6–7

Dear God,
I live alone with myself so much of the time. No one knows what I'm thinking or worrying about. No one knows my little fantasies and secret insecurities. And no one seems to care nearly as much as I do about myself. Since I cannot hear you, I wonder too, if you know what is going on in this heart of mine. But then I read what Jesus said. You even know each sparrow, like the stripped sparrow that the Audubon Society says is 700 miles off track north of town right now. You know how he got here and where he will be tomorrow along with every other sparrow in the whole entire world. You have not forgotten me, and you know my heart. What's more is that you love me. That blows my mind because I don't love me, not like that. I love me in a selfish way. You love me in a pure and encouraging way. Thank you for leaving behind these words of love and grace, "You are of more value than many sparrows." Today I will smile to think that you see each thought and know each word before it leaves my mouth. AMEN

We are never alone, not for one second. Let that thought make you flit around like a sparrow.

Additional Reading: Psalm 139

SEPTEMBER 28

You have searched me, Lord, and you know me. You know when I sit and when I rise; you perceive my thoughts from afar. You discern my going out and my lying down; you are familiar with all my ways. Before a word is on my tongue you, Lord, know it completely.
— *Psalm 139:1-4*

Dear Heavenly Father,
So often I wonder if I am alone. I cannot see you and I have never heard your voice. But then I see in your word that you are intimately involved in every move I make. You see me all day and all night. You know my thoughts and words before I do. I find comfort in knowing that you know me so well. I cannot hide anything from you. Help me to remember that when I'm tempted to sin or to doubt your loving care. You knew everything about me and still chose to redeem me in your Son. How can that be? It's what makes you so amazing to me. I want to make you happy with my thoughts, words and actions. Help me be pleasing in your sight today. Give me someone new to encourage as well.
AMEN

God is always present whether we acknowledge him is the only contingency.

Additional Reading: Numbers 11

SEPTEMBER 29

Cast all your anxiety on him because he cares for you. – 1 Peter 5:7

Dear Heavenly Father,
How much energy I have wasted by worrying over my own lot in life or that of my loved ones. So often the bad things that I fear never happen and what looks bad you always turn for my good and the good of others. Furthermore, you often bring blessings into my life, more than I could ever imagine. Today I will listen to your word! I give you each of the things I have been fretting over. (List them here.) Since I won't be worrying so much, I will give myself to doing more productive things, like helping others in your name. Show me today someone I can help. And give me the energy to act on my thoughts and make it happen.
AMEN

Without worry, we are free to grow and go in ways we never imagined.

Additional Reading: Isaiah 41:10

SEPTEMBER 30

Do everything without grumbling or arguing, so that you may become blameless and pure, "children of God without fault in a warped and crooked generation." Then you will shine among them like stars in the sky as you hold firmly to the word of life. – Philippians 2:14-15

Dear Jesus,
You lived 33 years, and never once did you grumble. I'm not sure I can go 33 minutes without grumbling to myself. I'm grateful that your life covers mine. But I see what you are saying. When I live out my days cheerfully, then I shine in front of a world darkened by selfish grumbling. I want the music of my life to match the words I hold out to them. Come by your Holy Spirit and exchange my poor pitiful grumbling with your cheerful, faith filled joy. Make my life a blessing to those who need to be cheered up today.
AMEN

Anyone can grumble in the face of adversity. Keeping a cheerful spirit is the real accomplishment.

Additional Reading: Numbers 11

OCTOBER 1

Surely I am with you always, to the very end of the age.
— Matthew 28:20

Dear Jesus,
When I was a little child, I always felt safe when I knew my Dad was around. When I was in school, I always behaved better when I knew the teacher was in the room. When I was in high school, I always had more fun when my closest friends were with me. When I have my family with me now, I have a hard time feeling lonely. All these blessings come from you sending someone to be with me! And then I read your words, "I will be with you always." You are all those people in my life; the One who makes me feel safe, who changes my behavior, who makes life more fun, who keeps me from feeling lonely. I need you every hour to be with me. Thank you for promising to be right here with me during this whole day. I know today will be good, because today you will be with me. Thanks.
AMEN

Jesus never intended for us to feel alone. We do that to ourselves.

Additional Reading: Joshua 1

OCTOBER 2

Speak up for those who cannot speak for themselves, for the rights of all who are destitute. Speak up and judge fairly; defend the rights of the poor and needy. Proverbs 31:8-9

Dear Jesus,
Right here in your word you tell me that I am my brother's keeper. You do not want me to get so lost in all my troubles and aspirations that I cannot see the needs of others around me. Help me to speak up for those in need in all circumstances. Help me to be a peacemaker between others and one who networks for the benefit of my friends and acquaintances. Open my eyes to see what you see. When it hurts to look at the poverty around me, give me courage to overcome my own wincing, roll up my sleeves and relieve the pain if even in a small way. You healed people that you knew would suffer again. Help me to do the same.
AMEN

Serving the needs of another springs from the center of Christ's heart.

Additional Reading: Acts 9:36-43

OCTOBER 3

I answered, "Sir, you know." And he said, "These are they who have come out of the great tribulation; they have washed their robes and made them white in the blood of the Lamb. – Revelation 7:12

Dear Jesus,
Funny how you describe life on earth as "the great tribulation" and I spend so much energy trying to make it feel like heaven. Why am I so surprised when daily life gets hard and troubles come? You consigned the world to this as our chastisement for our sin. Instead of making this heaven on earth where we all live in sin forever, you came, and you lived, and you shed your blood on that great and horrible day. It was your "great tribulation". Here, wash my life and make it white in your blood. And reserve for me a place standing before your gracious throne where there is no more tribulation, trouble or sorrow. Since I am going there to be with you in righteousness forever, help me to live with hope, joy and peace no matter what I am facing today.
AMEN

"True hope comes as a gift from God's good news and nowhere else."

Additional Reading: 1Peter 1

OCTOBER 4

Still another said, "I will follow you, Lord; but first let me go back and say goodbye to my family." Jesus replied, "No one who puts a hand to the plow and looks back is fit for service in the kingdom of God."
—Luke 9:61-62

Lord Jesus,
Lately we have had to remind our son to tell us what he is doing when he takes off to be with friends. He can get so excited to be with friends that he forgets to communicate with his parents. In that context I understand what you were saying to that fellow who wanted to follow you but first wanted to say "goodbye" to his family. You want us to be so excited and faith filled that when you call on us to follow you, that we drop everything and everyone to be near you. I know you are God and I know that you give me eternal life. I want to be near you more than everyone else. Help me to make time to be with you in personal devotional time. Help me to protect our time together with all my heart. And when I am with others, come with me and guide me so that in every place I am truly following you.
AMEN

Trying to follow Jesus and someone else is like "texting" while you're driving. Disaster looms.

Additional Reading: Matthew 6:19-34

OCTOBER 5

We love because he first loved us. – 1 John 4:19

Dear Jesus,
I love my parents because I realize how many great and wonderful sacrifices, they made to love me and my siblings. Their love for me has produced love in me for them. It's the same with you. Not until I realized what great love you have given me by making me and putting me in your world, did I really have any feelings for you. And not until I realized the great sacrifice you made for my forgiveness and redemption did, I have such strong feelings of attraction to your name. But I love you now more than ever. Help me to do the same for others by loving them first. Help me to produce love in them by NOT waiting for them to show any feelings for me before I reach out to touch their lives. And when they do notice that I have loved them with the kind of love that you have shown me, prevent me from exploiting that love and using it to manipulate them into liking me. Give me the ability to simply tell them about how it was really your love flowing through me all along.
AMEN

Loving another person first, takes faith in God and faith in the power of his love.

Additional Reading: Romans 12

OCTOBER 6

As they were walking along the road, a man said to him, "I will follow you wherever you go." Jesus replied, "Foxes have dens and birds have nests, but the Son of Man has no place to lay his head."
— Luke 9:57-58

Dear Jesus,
You lived your whole earthly life without ever settling down and making it home. You weren't at home. Home for you is heaven where all the angels praise you and understand the grandeur of your love and holiness. Our dimwitted human race sees you only through the fog of our fallen reason. How could you ever feel at home among us when we struggle so much to "get" you? But you still came and loved us perfectly. You left home to love lost souls. Help me to leave my "den" to love lost souls just as you did. If my comforts keep me from saving a soul, I will despise that comfort. Relive your life through me until my last breath here. Then I will be home with you.
AMEN

This is not our home.

Additional Reading: 2 Corinthians 5

OCTOBER 7

So then, those who suffer according to God's will should commit themselves to their faithful Creator and continue to do good.
– 1 Peter 4:19

Dear Heavenly Father,
I spend my whole life trying to avoid suffering. If I feel pain, I do whatever I can to get rid of it. If I sense a conflict in a relationship, I tend to shrink back to protect myself from emotional pain. If I see struggle and work coming my way, I think of how I can hurry up and get past it. I'm naturally wired to avoid pain. And then you say in this verse, "those who suffer according to God's will ..." How foreign the idea is to me that you would will my suffering. But to help me grow, you lead me into suffering. I believe it. That's what your word tells me. Help me to continue having a good attitude even in suffering, to continue to do all the good I can for others even in suffering and to continue to glorify your name even in suffering. By your Holy Spirit give me the same maturity about suffering that your Son had when he willingly took up the cross for me.
AMEN

Job's suffering was "good" in God's eyes because it taught the devil a lesson. I wonder what my suffering is teaching him.

Additional Reading: Job 42

OCTOBER 8

Many are the plans in a person's heart, but it is the Lord's purpose that prevails. – Proverbs 19:21

Dear Lord,
I plan so many things for myself and my family. And sometimes I think that just because I make these plans that you and the whole universe should cooperate to make sure I get to see them to completion. How silly of me to think that I am the center of the universe and that all good plans start with me! I repent. You have purposes far beyond me and whatever my mind can conceive All of your plans lead to eternal survival too – for me and many others. Thank you for not always cooperating with my plans and give me that heart that wants to cooperate with your plans with joy and humility.
AMEN

Man proposes. God disposes. And then God re-proposes a new and better plan.

Additional Reading: Genesis 50

OCTOBER 9

On my bed I remember you; I think of you through the watches of the night. Because you are my help, I sing in the shadow of your wings. I cling to you; your right hand upholds me. Psalm 63:6-8

Dear Jesus,
Sometimes I cannot sleep because of the worries I have about my health or my loved ones. I try not to wake myself with my thoughts but sometimes they are too overwhelming. In those times I want to be like David who wrote above, "On my bed I remember You; I think of You in the watches of the night ... I sing in the shadow of Your wings." I know you love me and protect me and that you want to give me sleep. Help me to remember that your right hand upholds me and that I will not pass away one minute early. So many times, you have rescued me. You are worthy of my trust. Your gift of salvation alone makes me let go and trust you with everything else. Thanks for being there and help me next time I cannot sleep.
AMEN

Trusting God helps the days go smoother and the nights be shorter.

Additional Reading: Psalm 127

OCTOBER 10

For the eyes of the Lord range throughout the earth to strengthen those whose hearts are fully committed to him. You have done a foolish thing, and from now on you will be at war. – 2 Chronicles 16:9

Dear Heavenly Father,
I know your love for me is unconditional. You made and saved me by your grace. But there are times that I have neglected your word and grace and went off to "do life" my own way. I know that you discipline your children and I can see by what you said to Asa in the passage above that you will send me negative consequences for my sins. I trust you even when you must discipline me. I know you're using consequences to call me back to yourself. I'd rather suffer under your consequences than be allowed to run freely toward eternal judgment. Thank you for intervening in our lives with stern but loving rebuke.
AMEN

Santa Claus isn't watching anyone, but God is.

Additional Reading: Hebrews 4:11-13

OCTOBER 11

Though the fig tree does not bud and there are no grapes on the vines, though the olive crop fails and the fields produce no food, though there are no sheep in the pen and no cattle in the stalls, yet I will rejoice in the Lord, I will be joyful in God my Savior. – Habakkuk 3:17-18

Dear God,
I've always been amazed by Habakkuk's statement here. I'm so used to praising you for the blessings you send my way in the form or food, money, good health and a bright future. But Habakkuk says that even if all those things were gone, he would still praise you because you were his Savior. I do get glimpses of this kind of pure praise in my soul. But too often I feel like my praise must be purchased with some sort of worldly blessing. Forgive me for my shallow thankfulness Help me to rejoice deep in my heart that my eternal salvation is secure. And give me that joy that brightens the room, springing from the peace of knowing you and your final, wonderful gift of total rescue.
AMEN

If we have the one thing needful, then we won't be needful of much else.

Additional Reading: Luke 10:38-42

OCTOBER 12

Through Jesus, therefore, let us continually offer to God a sacrifice of praise—the fruit of lips that openly profess his name. And do not forget to do good and to share with others, for with such sacrifices God is pleased. – Hebrews 13:15-16

Dear Jesus,
I love being a Christian. I have peace in my heart. My sins can't bother me so much. I have love from you that helps me be a blessing to others, even those who work against me. I have access to your word that guides and protects my heart from huge silly, worldly mistakes too. But I don't always show others how happy I am to be a Christian. Instead, I hide my contentment under surface gripes and complaints about petty things in my life. Please help me to openly profess the joy I have because you have brought me to faith. Don't let me be weird about it. Just help me freely express how wonderful it is to be your follower.
AMEN

Joy springing from within during all circumstances is one of the most powerful witnesses to Christ in a world unable to find happiness on its own.

Additional Reading: 1 Timothy 6:2-10

OCTOBER 13

Then the Lord said to Joshua, "See, I have delivered Jericho into your hands, along with its king and its fighting men. March around the city once with all the armed men. Do this for six days. Have seven priests carry trumpets of rams' horns in front of the ark. On the seventh day, march around the city seven times, with the priests blowing the trumpets. When you hear them sound a long blast on the trumpets, have the whole army give a loud shout; then the wall of the city will collapse and the army will go up, everyone straight in."
— Joshua 6:2-5

Dear Jesus,
what crazy battle plans you gave Joshua. But you wanted your people to know that you were the One delivering the land to them and not themselves. Help me to remember this when you thwart my plans and take me in another direction that seems crazy to me. Help me to quietly trust your ways and move forward in the direction you lead. You call on me to trust your word and obey, when I have no way of seeing how my life will work out. Give me the faith to follow you in that great adventure. I know that if you did not spare your own Son for me, that you have blessings and not curses in store for me. Give me peace today so I comfort and encourage the people along on my journey instead of giving way to negativity and complaining.
AMEN

You can tell if you are willingly following the Lord, by the look on your face, the words in your mouth and the spring in our step.

Additional Reading: Joshua 4 and 6

OCTOBER 14

Whatever you do, work at it with all your heart, as working for the Lord, not for human masters, since you know that you will receive an inheritance from the Lord as a reward. It is the Lord Christ you are serving. Colossians 3:23-24

Dear Jesus,
So often I base my motivation to work hard at my job, in my family or at my church on the approval and praise of others. When I do that, I am forgetting about you. When I remember that you sent me into these callings and that you are watching me work and that you are the one at the end of the day that will settle all just accounts with me, then I am not so dependent on other people's encouragements or responses. My opinions don't have to be honored and my "perfect perspective" does not have to be accepted. I can be involved with all my heart even when I am not always recognized or followed. Help me to live for an audience of One! You and you only have my heart.
AMEN

Jesus and I will live this life of mine. Together we will serve you without regard for your response.

Additional Reading: Proverbs 9 especially verse 10

OCTOBER 15

Do not let anyone who delights in false humility and the worship of angels disqualify you. Such a person also goes into great detail about what they have seen; they are puffed up with idle notions by their unspiritual mind. They have lost connection with the head, from whom the whole body, supported and held together by its ligaments and sinews, grows as God causes it to grow. – Colossians 2:18-19

Dear Jesus,

I do not know anyone who worships angels like those people Paul mentions. But I do know some folks who go into great detail about the visions, dreams and subjective experiences they have had as Christians. Sometimes, I am led to crave the same supernatural experiences. But I see in your word that you are my head and that it's your words I need. As tempting as subjective experiences sound, they are really a fog that clouds my relationship with you and makes you hard to see. Protect me, Lord Jesus, from the desire to have faith in what I experience instead of faith in you as my Savior. In your teachings I have all the peace and joy I need for my soul. Keep me from the uncertain ground of experiential mysticism. And forgive me when I cannot tell the difference between authentic moments with your Holy Spirit and simple human psychological wanderings.
AMEN

Christ given faith trusts like Job. It trusts that God is there even though he is giving no indication to our five senses.

Additional Reading: Hebrews 11:1-6

OCTOBER 16

We always thank God, the Father of our Lord Jesus Christ, when we pray for you, because we have heard of your faith in Christ Jesus and of the love you have for all God's people — the faith and love that spring from the hope stored up for you in heaven and about which you have already heard in the true message of the gospel
— Colossians 1:3-5

Dear Lord Jesus,
Your word has created some wonderful people to surround me and keep me going. Just like Paul does in the verse above, I thank you for these people who have kept my faith strong by teaching me, modeling for me and mentoring me. (List the people you thank God for here.) Thanks to what you have done through them, I trust you more and I am learning to love people more unconditionally. And it all stems back to the gospel! You have saved me, and you have reserved for me a place in heaven. Since I know that I will survive every problem I have, I am free to focus on relieving the suffering of others. Thank you for the people you use to keep me free!

"I do not need so much to be freed from my problems as I do from my morbid curiosity with them."

Additional Reading: Psalm 133

OCTOBER 17

"Blessed are you when people insult you, persecute you and falsely say all kinds of evil against you because of me. 12 Rejoice and be glad, because great is your reward in heaven, for in the same way they persecuted the prophets who were before you. – Matthew 5:11-12

Dear Jesus,
It always feels so lonely to be disliked by someone. You knew that feeling your entire ministry on earth. You told us that you were not alone because your Father was with you. (John 8) Your words here in the last beatitude help me realize that you are with me too. When people speak against us Christians I can think, "Hey, I am good company." Help me keep the goal of glorifying your name in front of others instead of avoiding persecution. When it's time to take a stand, give me the strength to rise to my feet. Make me a bold witness for your gospel and a beacon for truth. Help me to care less about what people think of me and care more about how much they think of you.
AMEN

When we live for Christ, we will experience the same social challenges he did.

Additional Reading: Matthew 10

OCTOBER 18

Each heart knows its own bitterness, and no one else can share its joy.
— Proverbs 14:10

Dear Heavenly Father,
I find such great comfort in this little verse, because you are showing me that you understand how alone I feel at times. When I am hurting inside sometimes it seems like even the most well-meaning loved one cannot open the door of my heart and enter there where I am. Even when I am extremely happy, I can sense a tinge of solitary confinement because those that rejoice with me seem to force their words. This little jewel says that it is the lot of every human. I am not alone in being alone. Everyone else is too. Except we are not alone because not only do you understand, you also are with us in every moment, good and bad. Thank you for graciously staying with me and for telling me that you understand. Help me to find peace in you in my solitary life.
AMEN

You cannot be alone anywhere in the world since in God we live and move and have our being.

Additional Reading: John 12

OCTOBER 19

"Against you, you only, have I sinned and done what is evil in your sight; so you are right in your verdict and justified when you judge."
Psalm 51:4

Dear Heavenly Father,
I am amazed that after David committed adultery with Bathsheba and had her husband killed that he would say that he had sinned against you and you alone. I ask, "What about Bathsheba, Uriah and the nation of Israel?" But that just shows how dark I can be. I know that David knew he had sinned against them too. But he was admitting what I often forget to admit from my heart. Sin deeply hurts you. You care for me more than anyone else ever could. You have planned for me to live a godly life. And I have hurt you so deeply with my hard heart and cavalier approach to so many things. I am sorry. I am so sorry! According to your unfailing love please forgive me! (Pause for reflection on the cross.) Thank you that you love me in your Son. I could never survive without your grace!
AMEN

Repentance is coming clean with God for the deep sins of the heart and being cleansed by God's forgiveness from the deep grace in his heart.

Additional Reading: Daniel 9

OCTOBER 20

In him we were also chosen, having been predestined according to the plan of him who works out everything in conformity with the purpose of his will, in order that we, who were the first to put our hope in Christ, might be for the praise of his glory. – Ephesians 1:11-12

Dear Heavenly Father,
It blows my mind that from eternity you had my life and my salvation all planned out. When I first came to know Christ or at other times when I struggled to understand you – and then after much struggle I found an answer from your Word,–at those times, I often thought it all depended on me and my effort. But it didn't. All the while, you were working everything out so I could be safe in true Christian faith. Help me to remember this when I am perplexed about things around me now. Help me to remember that you are working things out for me and others so each one of us will: come to faith, stay in the faith and land safely in heaven where will never get bewildered again. Holy Spirit, you can drive my emotions better than me. So, take over and steer me to frequent rest stops, please!!!!!
AMEN

Before time God planned out our eternal salvation, how much more the smaller details of our lives.

Additional Reading: Ephesians 1 and 2

OCTOBER 21

"Without wood a fire goes out; without a gossip a quarrel dies down."
– Proverbs 26:20

Dear Heavenly Father,
What a simple and clear insight you give me in this little proverb. When I hear a word of gossip all I must do is nothing. I just let the thought disappear buried in my soul. I can forget about it and make sure others never hear about it from me. I can kill the gossip like water kills a fire. So often I feel like there is nothing I can do about the gossip. But you are showing me that nothing is what I do. Then I will keep the forest fire from burning in my neck of the woods. Help me to replace gossip, once I have killed it, with words that reflect love and truth and lead others back to you. And thanks for forgiving me for all the times I stoked the fire instead of putting it out!
AMEN

Killing gossip is one of the most wholesome things you can do on earth.

Additional Reading: James 3

OCTOBER 22

"I the LORD do not change. So you, O descendants of Jacob, are not destroyed." – Malachi 3:6

Dear Heavenly Father,
I know that you are the just God of the universe who cannot watch me sin without pain and disappointment and a perfect need to judge my evil. I have often wondered why you have not brought great calamity on my life because of my many sins. But you are also the God of love and grace and you do not wish to slam down your just anger on me. You solved your own dilemma at the cross of your Son. You do not change! Always just and always grace at the same time. And so, I love you in humility and truth. I love you that you have confronted me with my sin to make me honestly own my failings. I love you because at the same time you have taken my sins away. I can be your own and live under you in true love and faith. I love you O God and I will give you my best today as an offering of thanks for never changing and always forgiving!
AMEN

To believe in God is to trust in his love that overcame his justice toward your own failings.

Additional Reading: Lamentations 3

OCTOBER 23

"Throw your net on the right side of the boat and you will find some fish." – John 21:6

Dear Jesus,
You must have had a smile on your face that day after your resurrection when you let your disciples fish all night without one fish and then appeared on shore and told them to throw their net on the other side of the boat. They caught lots of fish and you caught their hearts forever. You have captured mine too. You control everything in my life, the "good" and the "bad." Free me from the prison of thinking I am responsible for everything around me. I control very little. I barely know how to maintain what you let me control too. You put all my blessings in my net. To me you are greater than all your gifts. Help me to live in the joy of having you as my Savior and provider. Then I will smile at setbacks as much as breakthroughs. You send them both to bless me.
AMEN

"If Jesus leaves your net empty, don't fret. He is making room for the other blessings."

Additional Reading: Malachi 3:6-15

OCTOBER 24

"Who is wise and understanding among you? Let them show it by their good life, by deeds done in the humility that comes from wisdom."
— James 3:13

Dear Jesus,

It is easy for me to get angry when I think I have a better idea than my family or coworkers and they just don't recognize it. The more that time passes the more I am tempted to believe they are so foolish and hardhearted. But actually, I see from this passage that sometimes I am the hardhearted one. I am hardhearted to think that I can stew in anger and a surly spirit just because they do not see things my way. Help me Jesus. Help me to be peaceful and full of good deeds toward those who disagree with me while I wait for them to see it my way. And if I am seeing things wrongly, open my eyes to see it. Open my heart to accept the fact that I have been wrong and give me the strength to freely admit that I have been mistaken.
Amen

He is wise who actively loves him who is a fool without frustration.

Additional Reading: Micah 6:6-8

OCTOBER 25

"Peace be with you, as the Father has sent me, I am sending you."
– John 20:21

Dear Jesus,
On your day of resurrection you delivered the very thing we all long for, peace. You delivered peace with God the Father. Now I know he has reconciled himself to me by sending you. You have given me peace about my past. Now, I can see that you have been watching over the good and the bad to make me into the person I am today. I have peace about the present, you are with me and will help me with everything. I have peace about the future. It's all going to work out okay either in this life or the place you are preparing for me. I have peace! There is no other way to get this kind of peace apart from following you. And I love it! Thanks, from the bottom of my heart. Now, who is it you want to send me to. I will gladly deliver your peace to whomever is ready to receive it.
AMEN

If someone says they have peace apart from Christ, they are either lying or woefully ignorant about what they will soon face.

Additional Reading: Hebrews 13:20-21

OCTOBER 26

"And I pray this: that your love will keep on growing in knowledge and every kind of discernment, so that you can approve the things that are superior and can be pure and blameless in the day of Christ, filled with the fruit of righteousness that comes through Jesus Christ to the glory and praise of God." – Philippians 1:9-11

Dear Jesus,
I want to grow in faith and love and discernment, so I can tell right from wrong in my heart long before I must decide what to do. I want my life to reflect a righteousness that comes from faith and love and not from rules and policies. It is no longer good enough for me to do the right thing. I want to do the right thing for the RIGHT reasons. I want to want to do the right thing naturally. So, make my love and faith grow by reminding me of you and your life inside of my life. Draw me back to your gospels and show me the way to live in my context and among my generation. Make me into a person who shows others what you are like every day without even a word.
AMEN

To grow in love and the knowledge of God is worth our wholehearted devotion.

Additional Reading: Ephesians 3

OCTOBER 27

"Go to your brothers and tell them that I am returning to my Father and your Father, to my God and your God." – John 20:17

Dear Father in Heaven,
Your Son called you my Father too. That means you treat me like you did Jesus. That means all of my life has meaning, even those things that seem meaningless to me, which by the way is an awful lot. Thank you for caring about me so much. Thank you for giving me challenges to go along with successes. Thank you for holding me up in those times I thought I was doing all the work. Thank you for loving me enough to correct me when I am wrong and to draw me back to your arms when I am wandering. Help more people to know that your only begotten Son has removed your justice so they can be your children too. I will try to help by telling them about you and Jesus. Now, I will charge out to meet the day you have given.
AMEN

When you know God is behind you as a loving Father, you can take on the world.

Additional Reading: Revelation 2 and 3

OCTOBER 28

On Monday of Jesus' last week, he went to Jerusalem and cleansed the temple of money changers and peddlers.

"As Jesus was cleansing the temple he said, 'It is written, "My house shall be called a house of prayer for all nations, and you have made it a den of robbers." – Matthew 21:13

Dear Jesus,
You showed your zeal for God and people to reconciled when you cleansed the temple on this day so long ago. You wanted people to be able to focus on their spiritual lives instead of commerce in church. Help me to focus on my spiritual life too. You knew that the temple folks were so entrenched in their worldliness with a religious veneer that they would react with hate and disgust for you if you did it. But it is didn't stop you. Give me the same zeal to protect and promote spiritual growth for all people. I want people to be reconciled to you, to know the power of your love in their lives. Also, give me the zeal to protect my own devotional time so I can keep the temple of my body cleansed from robbers who would destroy my soul and the peace you have given it.
AMEN

"Since our bodies are the temple of the Holy Spirit, how should we keep them spiritually clean?"

Additional Reading: John 4:1-26

OCTOBER 29

On Tuesday of the last week of Jesus' life he taught all day in the temple court he had cleansed of the merchants the day before.

Jesus replied to the Sadducees, "You are in error because you do not know the Scriptures or the power of God." – Matthew 22:29

Dear Jesus,
In your answer to those men who taunted you with questions, I find the secret to many of my spiritual problems. My own ignorance of your Holy Word keeps me from understanding so many things. And my lack of experience with your power to take care of all things for me leaves me thinking I must be all sufficient for every challenge. Please, give me that drive to explore your word every chance I get and show me your power to take care of me and those I love. I do not want to be an ignorant wanderer who questions everything. I want to know what you have for us. Thank you for putting a book on earth where I can hear you talking to me.
AMEN

No personal daily habit can give you more strength than daily spending time feeding quietly on God's word.

Additional Reading: Psalm 1 and Psalm 119

OCTOBER 30

"A fool has no delight in understanding, but in expressing his own heart." – Proverbs 18:2

Dear Lord Jesus,
I often find myself scheming on how to make myself understood by others. I want them to know me, my passions, my purposes and my perspective. Less often do I seem to want to know them, their passions, their purposes and perspectives. I repent. Help me to ask thoughtful questions and to thoughtfully listen to what people are trying to say to me. Make me a person of understanding who draws out the real person deep down inside of others. Help me to love them for who they are, to understand them in the way they think and to shed your light of truth on those places where they need it. And when they shed the light of truth on my heart, help me not to run for cover but to courageously listen and adjust whatever you might be telling me through them.
AMEN

It takes courage and love to really understand another person.

Additional Reading: Proverbs 16:21-24

OCTOBER 31

"My goal is to know Him (Jesus) and the power of His resurrection and the fellowship of His sufferings, being conformed to His death."
– Philippians 3:10

Dear Jesus,
My mind and heart gets filled with goals every day and often the goal I see in this passage is only one among many. Then when trouble comes, I chaff and complain inside. I want to know the power of your resurrection living in my heart, how I can live above my world around me? How I can refuse sin and evil and fear of suffering? How I can have hope in all situations? When I see Paul's words that he wanted to fellowship in your sufferings, it is foreign to my mind. Help me Jesus, to want to serve God's will, "come what may" so that my life reaches its full potential in your eyes, even if that means death. I entrust my life in your hands.
AMEN

We do not live until we die to our desire to ourselves.

Additional Reading: Matthew 16:24-28, John 12:24-26

NOVEMBER 1

Luke 15:20 So he got up and went to his father. "But while he was still a long way off, his father saw him and was filled with compassion for him; he ran to his son, threw his arms around him and kissed him.

Dear God,
Everyone loves happy endings. So was the case for this son. The ending is happy not so much that the son humbly admitted his wrongdoings and was happily reunited with his father. The ending is happy because the Father was still waiting for his foolish, rebellious son. The ending is happy because the Father was waiting to reinstate his son as a son in full standing. Day in and day out, from one year to the next, I find your arms open and feel your loving embrace when I come to you in prayer and when I listen to your Word. Thank you for still waiting for me although I often wander from home. Thank you for watchful eye and heart full of compassion.
Amen.

I look forward to a happy ending with Jesus every day.

Additional Reading: 1 John 3:1-3

NOVEMBER 2

"Be compassionate and humble, not paying back evil for evil or insult for insult but, on the contrary, giving a blessing, since you were called for this, so that you can inherit a blessing. – 1 Peter 3:8-9

Dear Jesus,
When I am slighted or someone pulls out in front of me to get ahead, the first thought I usually have is not, "Don't be a proud self." It's, "Hey, that guy is wrong and of all people he should not have wronged me!" Then I sometimes say insults under my breath. Help me to change that. Help me to give a blessing and to be humble not expecting any special treatment. I want to learn to smile from deep in my heart and wave at the irritation I want to overcome evil with good. Give me that wisdom and strength to bless and not curse when insults come. And in the family, help me to not be so comfortable with my spouse and kids that I spar with them needlessly over silly things.
AMEN

Control of the tongue begins with control of the heart, a fruit of the Spirit.

Additional Reading: Galatians 5:22-24

NOVEMBER 3

"'Look, I have been slaving many years for you, and I have never disobeyed your orders, yet you never gave me a young goat so I could celebrate with my friends." – Luke 15:29

Dear Jesus,
It's confession time! The words you put into the mouth of the older brother (in the parable) to show your friends how they sounded before God when he was giving his grace to sinners; they convict me. Too often I view my service to you like that of a spiritual "employee." I think of what's in it for me and measure how you have blessed others compared to me. I forget that we have a loving, lasting family relationship. I am your child and you have promised to give me everything I need for this body and life. I repent of being so selfish. Now help me to throw myself into loving you and serving others. I want to lose my life so I can find it again. AMEN

Taking stock of one's own blessings compared to others, lowers the value of each share.

Additional Reading: 2 Corinthians 8 and 9

NOVEMBER 4

"Love never fails." – 1 Corinthians 13:8

Dear Jesus,
Though such a short passage, it speaks volumes in my heart. Love never fails. I think of the people from whom I want to walk away, and I ask, "Never?" I think of the worst sinners who hurt so many people, and I ask, "Never?" I think of the repeated sarcastic remarks and failures to come through in a pinch and I ask, "Never?" Can we not just once give up loving those who declare that they despise our love?" But your love, even in justice, never fails. I want that love that makes me pursue the lost, the mean, the twisted to give them one more opportunity to be restored. Give me that love by your Holy Spirit. Use the gospel story of your cross to melt my hard heart and teach me how to love even when I must confront or draw boundaries. Free me from my fickle heart!
AMEN

Love dares to keep pursuing another soul even though it runs away from such love.

Additional Reading: John 21

NOVEMBER 5

"There is rejoicing in the presence of the angels of God over one sinner who repents." – Luke 15:10

Dear Jesus,
You said this when you had to defend yourself against criticism for sitting with those who had spent a lifetime hurting and rejecting others. Sometimes it seems to me to be such a huge waste of time to sit with people who have made such a huge mess out of their lives. But you press me into it because you and all the angels of heaven are wanting those souls to turn back and be saved. Help me to not keep thinking about how much they have offended me or others and to just focus on how badly you want them back in your fold. I want to learn to rejoice over a sinner saved more than sulk over the damage they have done. Help me Lord Jesus to deal with the Pharisee in my heart.
AMEN

To forgive is to free both me and the one who has hurt me.

Additional Reading: Luke 15

NOVEMBER 6

"If two lie down together they will keep warm, but how can one be warm alone?" – Ecclesiastes 4:11

Dear Heavenly Father,
Today I thank you for all the friends you have put into my life who were there when I needed them, who confronted me honestly when I was acting out of my mind and apart from your truth and grace, who picked up the slack I had created, who loved me when I was unlovable, who trusted me with their secrets, who set aside their schedule to dry my tears or listen to a grief observed, who allowed long lunches, slow walks and quirks that I could not avoid. Thank you for the friends who took time to call for no reason at all and who dared to share life with me of all people. Help me to be that friend that you have given me, so I make other's lives more pleasant, tolerable and wonderful. Jesus, help me lay down my life for my friends like you!
AMEN

In Friendship we multiply one another's joys and divide one another's sorrows.

Additional Reading: Romans 12

NOVEMBER 7

"Let us not grow weary in doing good, for at the proper time we will reap a harvest if we do not give up." – Galatians 6:9

Dear Jesus,
Give me the faith and patience to wait for the proper time for you to produce a harvest from the good deeds you lead me to do. I sometimes want immediate results and grow disappointed and impatient and even want to quit doing those things. Help me to stop trying to be you, oh God. You decide what results you are working in all that you lead us to do. I just want to be your instrument. You can be the author and finisher of what I do. Give me the will to do good for everyone today and to throw results to the wind.
AMEN

Give much thought to whom you might help. Give little thought to how they respond.

Additional Reading: Mark 4:26-29

NOVEMBER 8

"Each one should test his own actions. Then he can take pride in himself, without comparing himself to someone else, for each one should carry his own load." –Galatians 6:4

Dear Jesus,
Your verse from Galatians is very insightful for me. You have uniquely suited me to live my own life with you. I know that no one can serve exactly like me nor can I serve like them. Often, I get distracted by what others are doing and want to compare myself to them to see how I am doing. Help me just to test my own thoughts and motives by filtering them through your word. Help me to love others but not compare myself to them. I want to be happy and content with my own life of love without measuring it by other people's abilities or interests. Also, thank you that you loved me before I showed any worthiness. Your love for me gives me stability and peace.
AMEN

We live for an audience of One.

Additional Reading: Genesis 4

NOVEMBER 9

However, I consider my life worth nothing to me; my only aim is to finish the race and complete the task the Lord Jesus has given me—the task of testifying to the good news of God's grace. –Acts 20:24

Dear Jesus,
You raised up a giant of a man when you made Saul into Paul (Paul means "small" or "humble"). The fact that he could honestly say that his life was nothing to him when he addressed the Ephesian elders while he was on his way to Jerusalem fully knowing he'd be arrested and sentenced to death, amazes me. Every day, I think about staying alive for as long as I can. In fact, I spend so much time thinking about how to stay alive that I neglect thinking about why I would want to lose my life for the sake of your gospel. My soul is safe, and heaven bound. Help me to throw myself into godly living and gospel outreach without worrying about how long I stay on this sinking ship. Give me the peace of faith-filled abandon from concern.
AMEN

Faith leads us to spend our lives, not save them.

Additional Reading: John 12:24-26, Acts 21:13, Titus 4:7, 1 Corinthians 4:7-12

NOVEMBER 10

"Today you will be with me in Paradise." – Luke 23:43

Dear Jesus,
I think of how frail and mortal I am. I won't be here long. And therefore, my body will not last. But I relish the words you told the thief next to you as you were making all things new, "Today Paradise." You have rescued me and so my soul and body will squeeze through death unscathed. I fear death at times, more than I want to admit. But having your promise of life, gives me a light to hold onto. As we enter Lent help me to be serious about life and faith and joyful about eternal life. And help those who preach, to give their people your heart and soul as they speak the very words of God.
AMEN

To live in Christ it to live beyond any earthly fate.

Additional Reading: Revelation 7:9-17

NOVEMBER 11

"When they hurled their insults at him, he did not retaliate; when he suffered, he made no threats. Instead, he entrusted himself to him who judges justly." – 1 Peter 2:23

Dear Jesus,
The way that you conducted yourself during your intense suffering is incredible. You trusted God under it all and that kept you from retaliating. And sometimes when I get the least bit of negative tone from another person, I shoot back the same to them. Please help me trust the Father the way that you do. Help me let go of the need to be respected, to be treated fairly, to always want others to be nice. Help me to trust that the Father is working out good even in their mistakes that affect me and then to let go of all need to control their responses. I want to reflect that love and trust that you used to save my soul. Perhaps I will save theirs too by getting an audience for your word once they seem my unique reaction caused by you.
AMEN

Living out the faith is impossible without the one in which we have faith.

Additional Reading: 1 Peter 3

NOVEMBER 13

"How great is the love the Father has lavished on us, that we should be called children of God! And that is what we are! The reason the world does not know us is that it did not know him." – 1 John 3:1

Dear Heavenly Father,
The family in which I grew up is unique. We all have a similar look, a similar sound and the same general outlook on life that was imprinted on us by two active faithful parents. We are like one other but different from so many others. I find it is the same for me in your Christian family. Your imprint on me has made me like my Christian friends but very different from this world. I have peace, security and purpose because you have redeemed me and made me your child. I don't have to fight for these. They are already mine. Thank you for adopting me. Help me today to enjoy the sublime truth of knowing I am your child and heir. Give me the outlook on everything that factors in your fatherly loving concern for me. Keep me positive and encouraging.
AMEN

Being a child of God brings so much more security than resting on any of our own accomplishments.

Additional Reading: Galatians 3

NOVEMBER 14

Galatians 5:22 – But the fruit of the Spirit is…patience.

Dear Jesus,
Patience is a virtue that does not come naturally. Ever since I was baby, I have wanted what I wanted right now! I need your Holy Spirit and the insight he brings – that waiting on you to order my life is better than pushing everything and everyone to give me what I think I need right away. Help me to be patient from deep down in my heart. Help me to remember that the plans you worked out for people like Old Testament Joseph, David and Abraham were wonderful once they reached their completion. I want to be patient and loving while I wait for your plan to unfold. Give me that peace which makes me smile when frustrations come.

To be truly patient in the face of life is a miracle worked by God.

Additional Reading: James 4:7-12

NOVEMBER 15

All the believers were one in heart and mind. No one claimed that any of his possessions was his own, but they shared everything they had. With great power the apostles continued to testify to the resurrection of the Lord Jesus, and much grace was upon them all. There were no needy persons among them. For from time to time those who owned lands or houses sold them, brought the money from the sales and put it at the apostles' feet, and it was distributed to anyone as he had need.
Acts 4:32-35

Dear Jesus,
We long to experience the kind of community that you created in that early church. We want to share everything. We want to be one heart and mind as we do life together. We want to be close friends and have close friends. Often our own crazy thinking gets in the way. We do things that distance others without even realizing it. Help us overcome our spiritually odd selfishness and to be simple hearted, generous and sharing with one another. Give us the love you have that gives more freely than anyone else so that we learn to power of losing everything for others so that we might gain everything for all. Today is our gift to you help us see how we can use it to make you smile!
AMEN

We lose only what we cannot bring ourselves to give away.

Additional Reading: Ecclesiastes 11:1-10

NOVEMBER 16

"But blessed is the man who trusts in the Lord, whose confidence is in him. He will be like a tree planted by the water that sends out its roots by the stream. It does not fear when heat comes; its leaves are always green. It has no worries in a year of drought and never fails to bear fruit." Jeremiah 17:7-8

Dear Heavenly Father,
I want to bear fruit in my life whether I am in hard times or good. I know that there is no way I can persistently bear fruit unless I remain close to you and your Word. Otherwise, my problems overwhelm me, and I become parched, dry and useless to everyone. Fill my mind with your words and nourish my soul inside, so that, whenever I experience trouble it cannot drain my emotional and physical strength. I trust you because you are my God and Savior. You have taught me to trust that you are always working good for me in everything. Thank you for the challenges I face and for the Word of your Spirit that enables me to meet them with a cheerful heart.
AMEN

The Word of God is living water that sustains a heart even in hard times.

Additional Reading: Psalm 1

NOVEMBER 17

"If I speak in the tongues of men and of angels, but have not love, I am only a resounding gong or a clanging cymbal. If I have the gift of prophecy, and can fathom all mysteries and all knowledge, and if I have a faith that can move mountains, but have not love, I am nothing. If I give all I possess to the poor and surrender my body to the flames, but have not love, I gain nothing. – 1 Corinthians 13:1-3

Dear Heavenly Father,
I get interested in pursuing many different things in life. I want more knowledge, better health, more wisdom, better living circumstances, a better job, more attention from others, less clutter, more freedom. To focus on these things threatens my happiness. But you want me to pursue love more than anything else. You want me to love you and people with all my heart, soul, and mind. While I know I will never be perfect at this love, I do want to make it my aim. Because when I pursue loving you and others, that's when I feel my greatest worth, my most peaceful place and I experience joy that no one can steal. Help me to love you and people faithfully the way you have loved me in your Son. Keep me from the viscous downward spiral of constantly thinking about how well I am loved or not loved by others and to persistently spiral up to loving people unconditionally.
AMEN

The True value of a human being has little to do with his accomplishments and a lot to do with how he loves.

Additional Reading: 1 John 4

NOVEMBER 18

My soul finds rest in God alone; my salvation comes from him. He alone is my rock and my salvation; he is my fortress; I will never be shaken.
— Psalm 62:1

Dear Heavenly Father,
I remember crossing a creek once and putting my foot on a large round stone, thinking it would hold me. But it rolled out from under my foot and I plopped into the water. That's the way I feel each time I try to make people around me to become my strength. Even if they hold me up or meet my needs for a time, sooner or later, they "roll" and I plop down in the "water". You really are the only rock for any of us. We can rest secure in your love and in your truth. Help me not to depend on others so much that I step on their hearts until they roll out from under me. Help me to have proper balance, being interdependent on others but not totally dependent on them. You are the only One on whom I can totally depend. And in this way keep me from getting so disappointed and angry if others let me down. I want to love them and help them even if they do not give me what I need. I know I can only do this if my heart rests fully on you. Lord, Jesus, you are my truest friend. Become the rock for my soul to depend upon.
AMEN

A soul resting in God blesses enemies and friends alike.

Additional Reading: Psalm 62

NOVEMBER 19

What is more, I consider everything a loss compared to the surpassing greatness of knowing Christ Jesus my Lord, for whose sake I have lost all things. I consider them rubbish, that I may gain Christ and be found in him, not having a righteousness of my own that comes from the law, but that which is through faith in Christ—the righteousness that comes from God and is by faith. – Philippians 3:8-9

Dear Jesus,
Every day, I ask myself how I'm doing. I think about the things I have done and not done. Sometimes I feel prideful that I'm not a failure like others. Sometimes I feel sad that I'm not a success like others. Either way, I don't really have peace about myself when I am thinking this way. Then, I look at this verse and think about what you have done. You have freed me from myself. I do not need to be anything other than a believer in you and your gift of righteousness. I'm free from trying to succeed to feel good about myself. Now, just help me to relax in your treasures and to honestly consider my personal accomplishments as "rubbish" compared to you. And help me live free from self-centeredness. Help me to throw myself into serving others out of love and not duty or ambition. I want to know the power of your love and righteousness guiding and strengthening my life.
AMEN

To live the Christian life is to live in and through Christ without thoughts about yourself.

Additional Reading: Matthew 6:19-24

NOVEMBER 20

"Therefore let everyone who is godly pray to you while you may be found; surely when the mighty waters rise, they will not reach him."
Psalm 32:6

O Lord,
As I juggle my busy schedule, I sometimes feel that I am treading water just to keep afloat. However, there are times when the harder I work the more I feel I'm sinking. Help me meditate on this Bible verse today. May I always remember that as I place all my problems and burdens on you, the waters will never overtake me for they can't overtake you. You keep me from sinking. I am never, ever alone. You displayed your ability to do this as you carried my burden of sin to the cross, and you will carry any other burdens I bear in this life. Continue to keep me afloat amidst the struggles I experience in this life. With Jesus as my safety device I pray. Amen.

God never stops checking his phone.

Additional Reading: Luke 18:1-8

NOVEMBER 21

"Love must be sincere. Hate what is evil and cling to what is good."
— Romans 12:9

Dear God,
You have made all of us with the amazing capacity to love. We can love you, people, pets, places, things, music and even concepts. Since our fall, it's so hard for us to discern good things from bad. So, we fall in love with people who are bad for us, or we fall in love with things and turn a cold shoulder to people. Or we love things that ultimately destroy us. We can also so easily turn from our spouse or family and love only people who don't know us so well and present themselves as someone easy to love. Please help me make my love sincere. I want to love the unlovable, to care for the lost, and the forgotten I also want to love unconditionally. I want to be like Jesus, who loved us all the same. He rejected the evil thought that we can chose to NOT love certain people. By your Holy Spirit, lead my heart to love purely all people and everything that is good for my soul, even if it causes trouble for me. Help me to love the people I am "stuck " with too. And help them to love me since they are "stuck" too.
AMEN

True love is given and taught by God through his Son. All other love is a cheap imitation.

Additional Reading: 1 Corinthians 13

NOVEMBER 22

"Love is patient" – *1 Corinthians 13:4*

Dear Jesus,
Some much is packed into those three little words, "Love is patient." I want everyone around me to change now for the better and especially when it affects me. If they do not change quickly, I grow impatient and want to push them with comments, body language and facial expressions that communicate, "Come on, get going and be better for me and everyone else!" I don't naturally want to be patient with anyone but me. Oh, please come and help me be like you. How consistently and patiently you bore with your disciples! You taught, modeled, restored, retaught and hung in there with them through their sluggish wanderings. Help me love people so much that I patiently wait for them to grow and learn without pushing them. Help me seek their best interest even when they are clueless about me and my needs. And help me enjoy doing all this without anger and frustration. Finally, help me see that what which makes me most impatient are those behaviors that I often exhibit myself.
AMEN

Being patient with someone is a win over one's self.

Additional Reading: 2 Peter 3

NOVEMBER 23

When you enter the land the Lord your God is giving you, do not learn the detestable ways of the nations there. – Deuteronomy 18:9

Dear Heavenly Father,
I know why you told ancient Israel not to imitate the practices of the Canaanites. It's because we humans are so weak that we look around us to see how we ought to live. We have darkened discernment and so we copy the culture in which we find ourselves. You have put me in this world, but you do not want me to be of this world. And I struggle with the materialism and self-centeredness of American culture. It's so easy to pursue worldly wealth as a sign of blessing, to guard my time for me and not serve others freely, to protect my entertainment instead of my neighbor's welfare. Help me to get out of myself, to focus on serving you and others and to shake off American "spoil yourself" values. Help me to live a life of sacrifice and giving and sharing and spending for you and others. Help me to shun immorality, to switch the channel and turn my face away from inappropriate commercials and to not laugh at sin or the breakdown of the family modeled on the screen. I do not want my family or me to mimic the world because I love you and the purity you have freely given me too much to drag it back through mud. Don't let me become a Canaanite!
AMEN

To do your best to avoid sin is a wonderful way to tell God that you love him.

Additional Reading: Jude

NOVEMBER 24

Luke 11:3 Give us each day our daily bread.

Dear Jesus,
You did not accumulate any great earthly wealth. And you lived in a very tumultuous economic time. Yet, we never once saw you worry and fret over your provisions. Instead, you focused on the needs of others, even our greatest need that would cost you the greatest price. Here you taught us to pray, "Give us this day our daily bread." What a volume of words! Daily, not even enough for two days. I see how you want me to live by teaching me to pray this way. Daily! God, take care of all my needs today and when you give me more than I need, pry my hands free from what I have so I will use it to meet other people's needs. Make me like you!
AMEN

It's not what you take with you but what you leave behind, that equates value.

Additional Reading: Deuteronomy 8

NOVEMBER 25

He who gathers crops in summer is a wise son, but he who sleeps during harvest is a disgraceful son. – Proverbs 10:5

Dear Heavenly Father,
At times I am tempted to be lazy and selfish. Instead of taking advantage of the opportunities you bring I can squander away time sitting in front of the TV or just doing nothing. Open my eyes and my heart to see the opportunities you give to make a brighter future for me and others. Help me to see how I can be happier spending my time making other people happy rather than focusing just on myself. And when it is time for me to spend a little extra time at my work to get the job done in a way that glorifies you, give me that strength and that spirit that makes me rise to the occasion and finish the job. All to the glory of your Son for what he did for me.
AMEN

For a Christian work to the glory of God is recreation.

Additional Reading: Ecclesiastes 11

NOVEMBER 26

Peter said, "Repent, then, and turn to God, so that your sins may be wiped out, that times of refreshing may come from the Lord, – Acts 3:19

Dear Jesus, when I hear the word "repentance" I often think of hard sobering thoughts. It is so hard for a sinner to repent. It is embarrassing, humbling and shaming. But Peter's words give me hope. When he called the people to repentance, he said it was so, "times of refreshing may come from the Lord." Help me to remember that you want to bring me happy, refreshing times but the door I enter to get into that room is repentance and not stubborn pride. Help me to readily say, "I'm sorry" to you and others. Search my life and see if there is any wicked way in me and lead me to repentance. Thank you that you refresh my life with forgiveness flowing from your cross, instead of condemning me when I admit my sins. AMEN

The greatest encouragement toward repentance is the knowledge that God loves to forgive.

Additional Reading: Romans 2

NOVEMBER 27

Do not be wise in your own eyes, fear the Lord and shun evil. – Proverbs 3:7

Dear Heavenly Father, the first sin revealed itself when Eve felt like she was wise in her own eyes. All too often I'm overconfident in my own thoughts and my own evaluation of things. Then I make judgments which I take back later. Help me to rely more on your truth and insights and not on my own opinions or those of other fallen people. I believe that you are watching everything that all of us is thinking and doing. Help my thoughts and actions fall in line with yours today. I want the people in my life to see you and your ways when they look at my life. In short, Father, I want to be like Jesus. Help me to grow into his likeness. AMEN

To want to be like God in holiness is a byproduct of faith.

Additional Reading: Proverbs 9

NOVEMBER 28

Therefore, since we are surrounded by such a great cloud of witnesses, let us throw off everything that hinders and the sin that so easily entangles, and let us run with perseverance the race marked out for us. Let us fix our eyes on Jesus, the author and perfecter of our faith, who for the joy set before him endured the cross, scorning its shame, and sat down at the right hand of the throne of God. 3 Consider him who endured such opposition from sinful men, so that you will not grow weary and lose heart. — Hebrews 12:1-3

Dear Jesus,
I want to finish the race of faith you have given me. But it is so easy for me to get way off track or to grow tired of the trouble it brings to run. Help me to remember the great saints of the Bible and those you have put in my life who have finished the race in the faith. Help me to draw insight from their lives, their successes, their failures and how you restored them. Help me to see you at the end of the race, scarred, smiling and cheering me on. I want to finish my life safely in the race of faith. Even thinking about you gives me strength to keep running. If you see anything in my life weighing me down, point it out to me, and give me the wisdom to throw it off so I can run faster and better toward the finish line. Keep me safe in the faith, Lord Jesus!
AMEN

Jesus ran the same race he asks us to run and he stands at the finish line to congratulate us.

Additional Reading: Psalm 119:32,33, Luke 13:24, 1 Corinthians 9:24-27

NOVEMBER 29

Nehemiah wrote, "There were many priests who signed the agreement to follow God's ways. I listed their names. But there were also doorkeepers, Levites, musicians and temple servants. They all gathered along with their wives and children to commit to following the law given through Moses 1000 years earlier. They committed to not give their children into marriage with non-Israelite people. They committed to keep the Sabbath Day rest laws, to cancel debts every seven years, to bring tithes, sacrifices and first-fruit offerings to the temple in a consistent and timely way. They committed to take turns supplying wood for the burnt offerings and to keep up the temple grounds to the glory of God."
– Nehemiah 10 paraphrased.

Dear Heavenly Father,
It's the nature of faith to make us want to glorify you in the way we support the ministry of the word. There is no temple anymore with its sacrificial demands. Your Son is the temple and his body is the church. But we still have church properties, clergy who dedicate themselves to our spiritual health and the spread of your wonderful news of forgiveness through your Son. I have benefited from this good news for many years. I have peace in my soul and my guilty conscience has something to cling to when the devil comes hounding me with my mistakes. I will support your ministry of the word with my money, my time and my unique abilities. I will "be there" for those laboring in your field. I will give with joy just as you have given to me. I want the world to know that you are a great God who restores guilty sinners and gives people a new lease on life every day. Oh Good, cause your people to rise up today in committed support of your gospel mission.
AMEN

The gospel is that something bigger than us that we can be a part of without regret.

Additional Reading: Nehemiah 10, Malachi 3

Donald W. Patterson

NOVEMBER 30

For although they knew God, they neither glorified him as God nor gave thanks to him, but their thinking became futile and their foolish hearts were darkened. – Romans 1:21

Dear Heavenly Father,
The verse above enlightens me on what humanity is like. By nature, we are futile in our thinking. We get lost in our own thoughts without any light of the reality of your truth and grace. We think of ourselves like gods, who made themselves, control themselves and bless themselves with wonderful things in life. In truth, we were made by you. We are preserved by you and everything we have is a gift from your hand. You decided who we would be and where we would live. So often in the futility of our own thinking, being thankful is miles away from our brain. Thank you, God, for everything. And please, please, forgive me for living without thankfulness so often. It's great to be alive, to be saved by your Son and to have meaningful work to do. Help me to beam thankfulness to everyone around me this week and always.
AMEN

Thanksgiving is a daily habit for those who know God.

Additional Reading: Psalm 145

DECEMBER 1

Finally, all of you, be like-minded, be sympathetic, love one another, be compassionate and humble. – 1 Peter 3:8

Dear Jesus,
You were kind and compassionate toward everyone you met. You never once fell into a selfish thought. You never once pulled back in disgust or froze someone out. You felt what they felt, saw what they saw and met their needs while neglecting yourself. You showed us what it means to live a godly life. It's a life that oozes love toward other people. I, on the other hand, struggle to love. But by your grace I can see what it looks like, and I can strive for it as my highest goal. But I need your help to be what you want me to be. Fill me with your Holy Spirit today so I see the needs of people and get excited about how I might be able to fill them. Make me feel what they feel and give me the wherewithal to help them. Then give me amnesia about what I did so I will say humble and ready for the next opportunity.
AMEN

Life is just plain more fun when you're serving.

Additional Reading: Ephesians 4

DECEMBER 2

Brothers, if someone you know is caught in a sin, you who are spiritual should restore him gently. – Galatians 6:1

Lord,
Help me to always remember that if someone I know is caught in a sin, that person still feels and hurts like everyone else. Help me to show the kindness and gentleness that you would show while I go boldly forward to show them the way back to you and your will. Don't let me sit idly by while they fall into grievous problems either. But get me going to speak the truth in love and to be as tenacious as Velcro as I fight for their soul. Help me to so value every person that I ache over their situation and hang in there with them. And please put people like this in my life,–people who are loving, gentle and outspoken to me so that they keep me safe from sin and every evil and so save my soul eternally.
AMEN

To have a friend who will patiently encourage you away from evil and back to God is to be rich.

Additional Reading: 2 Samuel 12

DECEMBER 3

When I heard these things, I sat down and wept. For some days I mourned and fasted and prayed before the God of heaven.
— Nehemiah 1:4

Dear Heavenly Father,
As I read of how Nehemiah mourned before you in prayer for several days after he heard about how your old holy city lay in ruins, I marvel that all too often I and my generation avoid true spiritual mourning at all costs. We are addicted to fun. And we keep ourselves from properly grieving the real tragedies of the world around us. Help me Father, to have the same heart Jesus had and let myself take time to grieve over "Jerusalem." Help me not to grieve over myself but for the needs of others that are not being met. And when I grieve, help me find peace in knowing that you are working it all out so that in the end I will see it all fixed in heaven. I love you Father and I know you love me. That will always be my peace even when I grieve.
AMEN

Be encouraged, God sees the same mess that you do.

Additional Reading: Nehemiah 1

DECEMBER 4

The Lord is righteous in all his ways and loving toward all he has made.
— Psalm 145:17

Dear Heavenly Father,
It's so easy for me to criticize you in my spirit. I sometimes think you are neglectful or cruel when I see the suffering of people and animals around me. Then I see in your word that you loudly proclaim that you are righteous and loving to all you have made. You have plans that are past finding out. Your disciplines for us creatures are good and yet at times they seem so unfair. Then I consider how sinful I am and how I deserve to be abandoned all together. Since you have not abandoned me but have run toward me in your Son, I will sit quietly and trust you. I will trust that you are good to me and all others and will wait to learn the meaning of our sufferings when you choose to reveal them to me either in this life or the next.
AMEN

The goodness of God needs no explanation. He turns all things for our benefit, whether we see it now or later in not important.

Additional Reading: Romans 11:33-36

DECEMBER 5

But who am I, and who are my people, that we should be able to give as generously as this? Everything comes from you, and we have given you only what comes from your hand. – 1 Chronicles 29:14

Dear Lord,
David was astounded that he would get to participate in your big temple project. He did not see it as a burden but as a blessing. Help me to see all the opportunities you give me to serve as a blessing and not a burden. Who am I that you should allow me with all my weaknesses to spread your precious words with people? Who am I that you would promise to make my money worth more if I invest in your movement on earth? Who am I that you would ask me to fit into your holy congregation and work with these people who are made saints by you? Melt my hard heart that so often selfishly complains and make me thankful like David. In Jesus' redeeming name,
AMEN.

To give offerings to the Lord is a privilege not a burden.

Additional Reading: 2 Corinthians 8 and 9

DECEMBER 6

Now when Daniel learned that the decree had been published (that no one could pray), he went home to his upstairs room where the windows opened toward Jerusalem. Three times a day he got down on his knees and prayed, giving thanks to his God, just as he had done before.
— Daniel 6:10

Lord,
I want to be like Daniel, resolute in prayer and my devotion to you no matter what threatens to interfere. When he was commanded not to pray, he just went right on praying. He loved you that much and knew you would bless him through it. I know you love me and will never leave me. So, I will do my best to not let anything (busy-ness, troubles, evil commands or good work) keep me from staying connected to you. And I humbly ask that you keep me on the right track in life by making your Spirit teach me in my heart every step of the way. I am so grateful that because you are driven by grace, you gladly pick me up when I fall and encourage me when I need it. Help me be like you to someone else today – forgiving and restoring.
AMEN

Let NOTHING keep you from your time with God.

Additional Reading: Luke 11:1-13

DECEMBER 7

I trust in you O Lord, ... you are my God and my times are in your hands. Deliver me from my enemies. – Psalm 31

Dear Heavenly Father,
So often I act like I am in control of everything about my life. Then when others threaten my physical, emotional or economic security, I get worried and scared as if it all depended on me. My times are in your hands and not mine. Help me to live with less stress because I recognize that nothing happens to me or my family that does not pass before your throne for permission. Help me to trust you and love those around me, even my enemies. Deliver me from anyone who would try to harm me, but also help me to love and forgive them so they will have an opportunity to see your love and grace before they face your throne of judgement.
AMEN

Let God have what is rightfully his – everything!

Additional Reading: Psalm 24

DECEMBER 8

So do not worry, saying, 'What shall we eat?' or 'What shall we drink?' or 'What shall we wear?' 32 For the pagans run after all these things, and your heavenly Father knows that you need them. 33 But seek first his kingdom and his righteousness, and all these things will be given to you as well." – Matthew 6:31-33

Dear Jesus,
You lived the life that mattered most for all people and yet you never had much of this earth's security and goods. You never worried about it either and in your words above, you tell me that I can live with the same kind of faith filled abandon. I am ashamed that so often when the car breaks down or a I lose my job that I worry and fret over where my help will come from. I am also ashamed that when my job is great and the economy is good, that I put my hope in those earthly things rather than in our heavenly Father. Thank you for grace. Now, help me to seek your kingdom and your righteousness for me and all those around me. Help me to put their spiritual welfare above my worries about providing for myself. I have our Father to take care of me. Give me what you want me to have and help me to want only what you give me. All for my good and your glory.
AMEN

Contentment is not getting what you want but is wanting what you have.

Additional Reading: 1 John 2

DECEMBER 9

By faith Abel offered a better sacrifice than Cain did. By faith he was commended as a righteous man, when God spoke well of his offerings. And by faith he still speaks, even though he is dead. – Hebrews 11:4

Dear Heavenly Father,
It was Abel's faith in you that made him give a sacrifice from the heart. He was not trying to earn your favor or simply go through the motions. He was giving his all for you because he loved you and trusted you. By listening to your word about Abel in Hebrews I want my life to be a living sacrifice to you. I want every part of my life to be an offering of thanks to you. By faith Abel's life still speaks to me today. Please help me to make good choices each day (based on my faith) so my life will speak good things to my family and friends long after I am gone. I do not want the memory of me to cause them to stumble or make them shake their heads. I would rather it make them strive to live closer to you. It was Abel's faith in you that made him give a sacrifice from the heart. He was not trying to earn your favor or simply go through the motions. He was giving his all for you because he loved you and trusted you. Help me live that way so after I come home to heaven, others' faith will be strengthened when they remember me.
AMEN

When your kids dig through your things for the last time, make sure they find some faith gems.

Additional Reading: Hebrews 11

DECEMBER 10

If we walk in the light, as he is in the light, we have fellowship with one another, and the blood of Jesus, his Son, purifies us from all sin.
– 1 John 1:7

Dear Jesus,
I long to have close personal fellowship with the people around me. But sometimes it seems so hard to achieve. Yet, you promise that as I learn to walk in the light of your truth and love,–and the people around me do to,–then I will have rich personal fellowship with them, the way you always intended people to have. Help us to walk in your light so we can enjoy close relationships. Help us live honestly, humbly and comforted by grace that covers all sins. Drive out all criticism and judgmental-ness so I welcome people with open arms. All of this so we can be close to you and one another and enjoy what the world hasn't got a clue about.
AMEN

Being close to God and others is an achievement of grace and not rules.

Additional Reading: 1 Peter 1:22-2:3

DECEMBER 11

We thank God continually because, when you received the Word of God, which you heard from us, you accepted it not as the word of men, but as it actually is, the Word of God, which is at work in you who believe."
– 1 Thessalonians 2:13

Dear Jesus,
You have sent so many people into my life to teach me your thoughts. When I let my mind drift back to my childhood, I think of all the Sunday School and Vacation Bible School teachers – they were all volunteers sent by you to teach my soul about who you are and how much you love me. I think of the faithful pastors, teachers in my schools, my parents and many friends who spoke up and out to me when I needed it the most. Help me always to regard the messages you send through others as your very words. And give me a desire to heed them and make them my anchor and guide. I would have never found you without these faithful missionaries for my soul.
AMEN

Thankfulness is the fruit of faith, dropping from a tree that has been well watered by the Master Gardener.

Additional Reading: 1 Thessalonians 2

DECEMBER 12

He who tends a fig tree will eat its fruit, and he who looks after his master will be honored. Proverbs 27:18

Dear Heavenly Father,
In this little proverb you are reminding me to take care of two very important things. I see you promise me that if I will 1) take care of the blessings you give me then I will enjoy the fruit of them the way you intended and 2) if I will honor and take care of those whom you sent to lead me (i.e. parents, bosses, pastors/elders and government leaders) then you will see to it that I am blessed to the max through them – How easily I stray from these simple little/big tasks and run after my own dreams. Please forgive me and help me to mind the business you have sent my way, all for Jesus' name's sake.
AMEN

Good works flow from faith and show themselves in everyday life.

Additional Reading: Genesis 24

DECEMBER 13

Put on the new self, created after the likeness of God in true righteousness and holiness. Ephesians 4:24

Dear Jesus,
Help me to face the week with my new clothes of your righteousness donned over my life. Help me to show the world what love and faith look like. When the temptations come to dress my heart like the world does, help me to say "no" to my old self and "yes" to my new spiritual self. And when I get it right, don't let be deceived by my pride that would creep in the back door of my heart. I love the peace from grace that you have given me. Help me to never lose it.
AMEN

Peace is knowing all things have been made right by someone who can keep it that way.

Additional Reading: Colossians 3

DECEMBER 14

Therefore, since Christ suffered in his body, arm yourselves also with the same attitude, because whoever suffers in the body is done with sin. 2 As a result, they do not live the rest of their earthly lives for evil human desires, but rather for the will of God. – 1 Peter 4:1-2

Dear Jesus,
You denied yourself all selfish desires and you could discern good and evil on a highly refined level. That made you keen to do everything God wanted you to do. You didn't miss one opportunity to serve others and you knew before anyone else that serving God meant dying early in a very tortuous way. I am so grateful for your perfect life and innocent death. Now, I need your help. I need you to help me arm myself with the same attitude that says, "I will serve God and others above myself." It's a real game changer, making me argue less and bless more. Oh Jesus, make me live for our Father's will more than anything else.
AMEN

When we decide to serve God before our day starts, then we know it will finish well.

Additional Reading: Mark 8:27-38

DECEMBER 15

You were taught with regard to your former way of life, to put off the old self, which is being corrupted by its sinful desires, to be renewed in your minds; and to put on the new self created to be like God.
– Ephesians 4:22-24

Dear Heavenly Father,
I know that I now have a new self in Christ. My old way of thinking and doing no longer has to be mine. Help me remember to put on the new self every day. You created that new self in me by teaching me your love and truth. I can unconditionally love everyone I meet, and I can stay away from selfish and unhealthy desires. I know that I can decide to follow you now that I have your Holy Spirit driving my heart. So, help me to be decisive and disciplined to live according to the grace you give. I want to shine today so others will know you through me. Help all my brothers and sisters in you to do the same today, so that we are a shining army conquering the world's darkness with the sword of light in your love and truth.
AMEN

Imagine our city luminated by hundreds of moving lights blinding those who live in darkness and showing them an alternative to their stumbling!

Additional Reading: Matthew 5:13-16

DECEMBER 16

Even if all fall away on account of you, I never will.
– Peter in Matthew 26:23

Dear Jesus,
Peter sums up the way I feel about my personal commitment to you. I know you are my friend and Savior and I feel like I will never fall away from you no matter what happens. But I know that Peter felt the same way and then he did fall away. He denied knowing you three times that very same night. And I see myself fall into sin the very same day I voice my devotion to you. We people are so weak and fickle. We are so easily distracted by our own sinful hearts or the devil. If it were not for you and your constant love I would fall away and never come back. Please keep me close by your Holy Spirit and be the power that saves my soul. I cannot save myself my own commitment. It's too weak. Help me to glorify you always.
AMEN

Strength is holding onto something strong.

Additional Reading: 1 Corinthians 10

DECEMBER 17

How foolish you are, and how slow of heart to believe all that the prophets have spoken! Did not the Christ have to suffer and these things and then enter into his glory? – Luke 24:25-26

Dear Jesus,
Don't let me be slow of heart to believe that what you did in your single solitary life was the fulfillment of all that the Old Testament prophets had foretold as well as the answer to all my fears and sorrows. You suffered to win for me freedom from my guilt, freedom from my fear of death, freedom from my inability to forgive others. Melt my stony heart and replace it with your powerful love fulfilled by your very life. Give me what I cannot produce on my own, faith, hope and love. Make me the person you always intended for me to be.
AMEN

Christ in us is the hope of glory.

Additional Reading: Romans 10

DECEMBER 18

O Lord and God, you deserve to receive glory, honor, and power because you created everything and by your will they are created and have their being. – Revelation 4:11

Dear Heavenly Father,
I exist because you invented me in your creative mind from eternity. You chose my gender, my parents, my siblings, my DNA, height, hair and eye color, even my raw intelligence was slotted by you. Thank you for thinking of me and then putting me into my place in your vast creation. I am sad too that I joined humanity in rebellion toward you and yet you redeemed me in your Son. Help me to live in thankfulness and praise today just as the creatures in heaven are praising you as I see from the Revelation passage above. I want to glorify you for the gift of life today in the way I live. Show me how to do that.
AMEN

God doesn't make junk so don't criticize the unchangeable parts of your life.

Additional Reading: Psalm 139

DECEMBER 19

We are his workmanship, created in Christ Jesus to do good works which He prepared in advance for us to do. – Ephesians 2:10

Dear Jesus,
Open my eyes to every opportunity to do good, for You have created me in Christ Jesus to do good works and have appointed in advance that I should walk in them. Give me a faithful heart for every task set before me. Grant me grace to serve all people as I would serve You my Lord. Help me to live this day as though you died yesterday, rose today and are coming back tomorrow. Make your cross be my glory and crown and make the thought of your return not intimidate me but stimulate me to earnest attention to my faith life toward you.
AMEN

To serve God and others is medicine for our souls.

Additional Reading: Esther 4

Donald W. Patterson

DECEMBER 20

Then the elders and all the people at the gate said, "We are witnesses. May the Lord make the woman who is coming into your home like Rachel and Leah, who together built up the family of Israel. May you have standing in Ephrathah and be famous in Bethlehem. Through the offspring the Lord gives you by this young woman, may your family be like that of Perez, whom Tamar bore to Judah." –Ruth 4:11-12

Dear Lord,
You gave Boaz, Naomi and Ruth, good friends who supported them and encouraged them with prayers and positive words. They were risking lots of things by living as servant leaders. The blessing of their friends must have helped their world make sense to them. Give me friends who will encourage and pray for me. Make me the kind of friend that encourages others and really prays for them too. Also, I see in this verse how you started to show your hand that it's not just a story, but it also shows us how you were protecting the ancestral line of your Son, our Savior. Thank you for showing your hand. It encourages our faith in your Saving work and redemptive heart.
AMEN

An encouraging friend is a rare gem ornamenting the committed life of any servant.

Additional Reading: Luke 24:44-49

DECEMBER 21

Concerning this salvation, the prophets, who spoke of the grace that was to come to you, searched intently and with the greatest care, 11 trying to find out the time and circumstances to which the Spirit of Christ in them was pointing when he predicted the sufferings of the Messiah and the glories that would follow. 12 It was revealed to them that they were not serving themselves but you, when they spoke of the things that have now been told you by those who have preached the gospel to you by the Holy Spirit sent from heaven. Even angels long to look into these things. – 1 Peter 1:10-12

Dear Jesus,
I sometimes forget just how fortunate we are to live right now in history. The Old Testament prophets got bits and pieces of prophecy, but you did show them the masterpiece of salvation in your Son that you have shown us in the gallery of the New Testament. The angels didn't even get to know your grand plan until we had seen it first. We are better off than the prophets and the angels. We know the entire story and it brings us great faith, peace and joy. It also gives us a clear message to share with our generation. Thank you for having set my life on this side of the cross. I feel privileged and deeply loved. When I start to have a pity party for myself, remind me of the great life in Christ you have created for me and turn me back to faith and love.
AMEN

No one understands the gospel about Jesus and trusts that God loves him apart from the miraculous gift of the Holy Spirit.

Additional Reading: I Corinthians 15:50

DECEMBER 22

So Boaz took Ruth and she became his wife. When he made love to her, the Lord enabled her to conceive, and she gave birth to a son. 14 The women said to Naomi: "Praise be to the Lord, who this day has not left you without a guardian-redeemer. May he become famous throughout Israel! 15 He will renew your life and sustain you in your old age. For your daughter-in-law, who loves you and who is better to you than seven sons, has given him birth." —Ruth 4:13-15

Dear Heavenly Father,
You turned a very bleak situation for Naomi into a blessing that is still read and appreciated today. You are the God who saves! This part of the story of Ruth reminds me of Easter when your Son rose from the grave. In Ruth and Naomi's lives you brought life from what looked like a dead end. Through Ruth you gave to Naomi what she thought she would never receive. Her family name and property were preserved and her place in history was riveted in print forever. Dear Lord, I hereby trust you with my story too. I know you will make the greatest good come out of every situation no matter how bleak or difficult. Help me to tie the knot of faith in the end of my rope when I come to it.
AMEN

With God the end is always better than the beginning.

Additional Reading: Isaiah 11:1-9

DECEMBER 23

In those days Caesar Augustus issued a decree that a census should be taken of the entire Roman world. 2 (This was the first census that took place while Quirinius was governor of Syria.) 3 And everyone went to their own town to register. 4 So Joseph also went up from the town of Nazareth in Galilee to Judea, to Bethlehem the town of David, because he belonged to the house and line of David. 5 He went there to register with Mary, who was pledged to be married to him and was expecting a child. —Luke 2:1-5

Dear Heavenly Father,
Would you really turn the whole Roman world upside down just to get your Son born in the town of David according to prophecy? Would you really make a man and woman endure suspicion the rest of their lives because you wanted them to have your baby? Would you really inconvenience us to accomplish your own will? How dare you act like God! I find it hard to believe that you would kick us off our thrones to accomplish your altruistic purposes, that is; until I realize this demonstrates how much you love everyone, my friends and my enemies. Oh, God! Do what you wish with our lives, so as many as possible can escape the awe-full justice awaiting their sins. Work your grace and save our souls at the expense of our childish and temporary dreams.
AMEN

God loves us too much to let us have everything we want at the expense of what we need the most.

Additional Reading: Malachi 3:1

DECEMBER 24

While they were there, the time came for the baby to be born, 7 and she gave birth to her firstborn, a son. She wrapped him in cloths and placed him in a manger, because there was no guest room available for them. —Luke 2:6-7

Dear Jesus,
It's so grand that I can hardly wrap my mind around it; the moment you were born, you were God lying there in the feed trough wrapped in rags. What a welcome we gave you and oh how similarly we have treated you throughout our lives. We say, "God you can be here with us," but we won't necessarily give you the honor and reverence you deserve. We give our "junk for Jesus" when our best gifts get cast down in front of idols. Thank you for being the patient and merciful Lord who died for roaches like us. I'm so thankful for your grace and by faith I will do my best to give you more than a manger as a dwelling place in my heart and life. Since you are here with all your blessings, I will be happy in my Christmas celebrations no matter what they do or don't look like.
AMEN

When Christ is in your Christmas it's always the best ever.

Additional Reading: Luke 1:26-38

DECEMBER 25

Believe in the light while you have the light, so that you may become children of light. —John 12:36

Dear Jesus, you have brought light into my otherwise dark life. I have hope in you that I could not find in the world. I have discovered that the world cannot replace it either. I am loved, I have purpose, I have destiny. I could never quite get any of this in the world. Your salvation has given it to me as the best Christmas gifts ever. And these gifts are my Christmas lights. Help me shine them brightly for friends and foes (and everyone in between) so they will be blessed with peace on earth through me. Also, help me be bold enough to tell everyone that the lights they see are a gift from you, a gift you want to share with them, too.
AMEN

The best Christmas lights come from Jesus himself.

Additional Reading: Matthew 5:14-16, Ephesians 5:1-20

DECEMBER 26

The LORD will not grow tired or weary. And his understanding no one can fathom. —Isaiah 41:28

Dear Lord,
You never grow tired of solving problems, of working a plan, or of listening to our prayers even when they are bad. You never grow tired of forgiving or helping us. I, one the other hand, live on the edge of exhaustion because I have such limited patience and energy. That's why I need you so much. You will hear my prayers and meet my needs. You have unlimited power and patience. Take all my concerns today and work your wonderful plan to reform me and shape me into the person you want me to be. Give me your supernatural strength to carry on in my path. And make me content in my corner of your world.
AMEN

God won't give you more than he can handle for you.

Additional Reading: Isaiah 40:13-14

DECEMBER 27

God gives strength to the weary and increases the power of the weak.
—Isaiah 40:29

Dear Lord,
I was born with a desire to be strong and invincible on my own power. I believe it is part of the root sin that Adam and Eve passed down to all of us. We want independent god likeness. But you know we are but dust. You see how weak and dependent we are and you promise to be our strength if we come to you asking in prayer. So, I'm coming to you now asking in prayer that you share your strength with me so I can deal with my problems, love people that need me and fight temptations. I need you in order to really live my life as I was designed by you to live. AMEN

There is only one God and he loves to share his strength with us little people.

Additional Reading: 2 Corinthians 12:9-10

DECEMBER 28

As long as it is day, we must do the works of him that sent me. Night is coming, when no one can work. While I am in the world, I am the light of the world." – Jesus Christ – John 9:4-5

Dear Heavenly Father,
Jesus, you always had a great grasp of the obvious. Time is nonrenewable so a person will want to live out their purpose in life 100% of the time and not, 98 % or 75 % or 25 %. How you must wonder at our aimlessness at times, how we fritter away days, weeks, months and years without discovering more truth, or sharing more truth with others or blessing those who need it. Now is our "daytime" on earth. Help us to work while it is day so when we are resting and enjoying heaven with you, the blessings we were here will be the great memories we reminisce about. Give me insight today on how to use my unique life to bless the most people possible.
AMEN

Be the blessing that only you can be for the people that have been planted next to you.

Additional Reading: Ecclesiastes 9:10

DECEMBER 29

I rejoiced greatly that I have found some of your children walking in truth, as we received commandment from the Father. – 2 John 1:4

Dear Heavenly Father,
I know you want us to live honestly believing the truth about you and the truth about us. My biggest problem is my own and sin and my biggest blessing is your grace. That's the truth. The truth is that you love me and that I am forgiven. The truth is that you are with me and want to lead me with your strength to be honest, humble, loving and forgiving with everyone. The truth is that you want me to approach every relationship as a servant and not as a master. You want me to dump my expectations of others and dream about how I might make their life better. The truth is you want me to be like your Son because your Son lives in me and wants others to know him. Oh, God of truth, help me to walk and live in the truth.
AMEN

It does not matter if there is truth if that truth does not matter to me.

Additional Reading: Ephesians 5:8

DECEMBER 30

And now I plead with you, lady, not as though I wrote a new commandment to you, but that which we have had from the beginning: that we love one another. 6 This is love, that we walk according to His commandments. This is the commandment, that as you have heard from the beginning, you should walk in it. –2 John 1:5-6

Dear Jesus,
Your Apostle, John, pleaded with his church that each member would love one another in faithful obedience to you. I want to listen to that plea with an open heart. I want to love every other person in my flock, in my family and in my life with a pure spiritual love that shows itself in forgiving helpfulness in every way. But my own hardness of heart gets in the way. I get calloused and flaky at times. Dear Jesus, crush my hard heart and help me deal with my weakness so I truly, actively love those around me.
AMEN

God's love is the most powerful force on the planet in relationships.

Additional Reading: Ephesians 5:2

DECEMBER 31

But do not forget this one thing, dear friends: with the Lord a day is like a thousand years and a thousand years are like a day. The Lord is not slow in keeping his promise to return, as some understand slowness. Instead he is patient with you, not wanting anyone to perish, but everyone to come to repentance. – 2 Peter 3:8-9

Dear Jesus,
You have graciously brought us safely to a new year. Every great saint, all the way back to the Apostle Peter, has felt that you would usher in the end of the world and judgement day in their lifetime. But here we are 2000 plus years later. It's easy to grow complacent and it makes skeptics believe their skepticism more. However, from Peter, we are taught what you are doing. You are being patient so more people will come to repentance. On my own I would be quick to judge but you love every soul, even the worst, much more than I do. It's amazing to me that you do not grow weary of our evil. It makes me more patient to see how patient you are with every human being. I'm glad that you are slow in judging. Otherwise, I would not be saved. You have shown great patience with me. Help me to stop counting time so that I can wait like you with a heart liberated by grace and living in view of eternity instead of time, especially when I see evil all around me.
AMEN

Sit and think about this for whole day; God does not want anyone to perish.

Additional Reading: Psalms 90:4